To Reap
a Bountiful Harvest

By Štěpánka Korytová-Magstadt

To Reap
a Bountiful Harvest

By Štěpánka Korytová-Magstadt

Rudi Publishing
Iowa City, Iowa

Rudi Publishing, 1901 Broadway, Suite 321, Iowa City, Iowa
52240

Dr. Robert West, Editorial Consultant

ISBN 0-945213-09-3

First Printing

PRINTED IN THE UNITED STATES OF AMERICA

Cover Photo: Threshing scene on the farm of Joseph Sudik, near
Schuyler Nebraska. 1893. Photo courtesy of Nebraska State
Historical Society.

Library of Congress Cataloging-in-Publication Data

Korytová-Magstadt, Štěpanká, 1956–
        To reap a bountiful harvest: Czech immigration beyond the
Mississippi, 1850–1900 / by Stepanka Korytova-Magstadt.
        p. cm.
        Based on the author's thesis (doctoral)—Charles University, 1991.
        Includes bibliographical references (p.   ) and index.
        ISBN 0-945213-09-3 : $24.95. — ISBN 0-945213-07-7 (pbk.) : $14.95
        1. Czech Americans—West (U.S.)—History—19th century. 2. West
(U.S.)—History—1848-1950. I. Title.
F596.3.B67K67 1993
978'.0049186—dc20   93-3364
                                                            CIP

Contents

Acknowledgments

I owe much to many people both here and in the Czech Republic—relatives, friends, and professors. My parents and friends gave me moral support, made suggestions, and corrected my English.

A few individuals and institutions deserve special thanks but, of course, have no responsibility for the mistakes and shortcomings of the book. The staff at Náprstek Museum in Prague helped me greatly in the research phase (thank you for all the cups of coffee!), as did Professors W. Chrislock of the College of St. Thomas, St. Paul, Minnesota, and I. Dubovický, J. Vařeka, and J. Opatrný of Charles University, Prague. In the archives at the University of Chicago I found important information with the help of Dr. Z. Hruban. J. Svoboda also helped a great deal at the University of Nebraska archives. I would like to express my gratitude to several former colleagues, particularly Professors M. Schuyler and T. Archwamety at the University of Nebraska at Kearney.

T. Boekhoff, publisher, and N. Ewald, editor, gave the book its present form, for which I am very grateful. What started out as a professional relationship between a publisher and an author blossomed into a friendship.

Last, but not least, this book would never have been written if it were not for two professors on either side of the ocean: J. Polišenský of Charles University, Prague, and T. Magstadt of the University of Nebraska. To both I owe a large debt of gratitude for their scholarly advice and moral support. Michael ("Misha") helped, too, but not in the same way—after all, there is only so much a baby can do.

Štěpánka Korytová-Magstadt

Kearney, Nebraska
March 13, 1993

Foreword

This book does not need a long introduction. It reads well and tells an interesting story, yet it corresponds at the same time to the demands of the now fashionable narrativist and epistemological historiography. It tells the tale of the Czech immigrants to the Great Plains states during the latter half of the nineteenth century and answers questions concerning the dates of their arrival, the places they came from and where they settled, and finally, it gives the character of the migration.

The Czechs used to be numbered only among the so-called "new immigration," arriving after 1883 or so. The author shows, however, that they were coming across the Mississippi-Missouri much earlier, usually via Chicago or St. Louis, especially after the Homestead Act of 1862. Even earlier, indeed, the first immigrants from Bohemia and Moravia came to the New World as early as 1530, and the first visitor to step on the soil of what is today Virginia was Joachim Gans, a mining expert from the Jewish quarter of the Old Town of Prague, who took part in the unfortunate expedition to Roanoke Island in 1585. Augustine Herrman was an esteemed citizen of New Amsterdam; the Jesuit missionaries from the Bohemian Province of the Company penetrated into New Spain as far as Arizona; and the members of the Moravian church settled in Georgia and the Carolinas before they finally found refuge in Pennsylvania. There they met Bohemian merchants dealing with glass and linen who had contacts with Benjamin Franklin.

But the first great wave of Czechs arrived after 1848, especially after 1852. Many settled in the great cities, but most of them were peasants who became farmers in Texas and Wisconsin. Gradually Nebraska became the state with the largest agrarian settlement of Czechs.

Štěpánka Korytová-Magstadt is the first historian of Czech emigration to the United States who has combined both the sources of the Czech archives and the results of American scholarship. From this point of view it is a pioneer work and a solid guide for those trying uncharted waters.

J. Polišenský, Professor Emeritus
Charles University, Prague

To my mom—mamce

Preface

In the medieval town of Kutná Hora, not far from Prague, where I grew up, stands the gothic Cathedral of Santa Barbara. This magnificent edifice, which rivals Prague Castle's famous Cathedral of St. Vitus in beauty, is the centerpiece of the former convent of Voršilky, which now houses the archives of the Central Bohemian District. When I visited the archives at Kutná Hora to do research for my doctoral dissertation, I did not realize the importance of this place in the history of Czech immigration to America.

An innkeeper by the name of Pospíšil left Kutná Hora, never to return, in 1845. Pospíšil, an early Czech, had no way of knowing what he and others like him had started. In the decades that followed, Czech rural population streamed out of Bohemia and Moravia—what started as a trickle in the 1840s became a torrent in the late 1880s. A century after this great wave of Czech immigrants arrived on the frontier, I stepped off a plane in New York City.

This book is about nineteenth-century Czech migration to rural America by a latecomer whose life has been directly affected by the descendants of those pioneers—people who became thoroughly American without forgetting who they were or whence they came. If it were not for my distant cousin, a Czech-American whom I met in Czechoslovakia, I would never have come to Nebraska or to the United States. Helping her find her roots in Czechoslovakia twenty years ago helped me discover a deep kinship between Czechoslovakia and the United States.

Soon after my arrival in Nebraska in 1982, I attended meetings of Czech-American clubs and, as the Czech-Americans gave me a warm reception, I ultimately joined one of the clubs. There was something peculiarly Czech about these Americans—not just the language, but the way they looked, the way they thought, even the way they felt (for Czechs, there is often a fine line between happiness and sadness). It was difficult to define, but I felt at home with these people. That feeling is not something that can be measured, but it is very real and it speaks volumes about the resilience of ethnicity and culture.

Being a historian, living in Nebraska, knowing the Czech and English languages, and coming into frequent contact with Czech-Americans and Czech-American culture, I realized that it was only logical for me to research the migration of Czechs to the rural United States. At first my interest was primarily intellectual. But, reading the memoirs of settlers in *Kalendář Amerikán*, I began to develop an emotional stake in this topic: the loneliness, isolation, homesickness, and pride in being Czech these early settlers expressed were mirrored in my own feelings. It was as though they were speaking to me in a very personal way from some distant place. We understood each other. It was comforting to know I was not alone. I was in good company. And so what started as an intellectual endeavor became an intensely personal one.

Once I left Czechoslovakia, I became a political refugee with no hope of returning. Nobody imagined in 1978, only ten years after the Soviet tanks had rolled into Czechoslovakia, that the political system would ever change. Certainly I did not expect that to happen in my lifetime.

In many respects, my journey to America was very different from that of the early Czech immigrants—and not simply in terms of transportation modes or time in transit. I was not "pulled" by opportunities in the West so much as "pushed" by personal and political circumstances. I just wanted to leave my homeland. My nineteenth-century predecessors left because they wanted a better life in "America" (it was not the United States *per se*, but the idea of *America* that evoked milk-and-honey images). They had a goal in mind. They also could not go back, mainly because they could not at first afford it, and later because they had so much invested (not only in a material sense).

When I began the research for this book, the political situation was highly unfavorable to the fostering of cordial relations between Czechoslovakia, my native country, and the United States, my adopted country. Now, with the research and the writing finished, the political situation in Czechoslovakia, Europe, and the world has dramatically changed. In 1989, the Berlin Wall came tumbling down, and shortly thereafter, Communist rule in Czechoslovakia tumbled as well. The impact of that change on the lives of all Czechs is immeasurable. That applies also to Czechs who have been in self-imposed exile—in some cases for four decades or more. In my case, it has meant that I am free to travel back and forth between the United States and Czechoslovakia without any obstacles, that I have been able to visit my family in Prague (and they too can now travel wherever they choose whenever they choose), that I could go home to have my baby, and that, in December 1991, I was able to earn the equivalent of a Ph.D. at Charles University in Prague, founded in 1348.

The history of Czech migration to the United States is a history of two countries on opposite sides of the Atlantic with interconnected destinies; beginning in the second half of the nineteenth century, the history of Bohemia and Moravia became fused at key points with the history of the United States. Then, after World War II, for reasons that are well known, contacts between Czechoslovakia and the United States were artificially interrupted for more than forty years. With the ending of the Cold War, a new era has begun in this long relationship.

It is my hope that the publication of this book will be a modest contribution to the renewal and strengthening of cultural and political ties between Czechoslovakia and the United States. Finally, I hope that the work will stimulate general interest not only in the ethnic and cultural history of Czechs in America, but also in my native country of Czechoslovakia.

Czech-Americans who visit Bohemia and Moravia now, even after all these years, often feel strangely at home in a place they have never been before. That is because people who stayed behind are the kinfolk, culturally if not biologically, of the people who left. In the same way, the people portrayed in the pages that follow are my people; they paved the way for me. The story of Czech-Americans—why they came and the trials they faced—is my story.

Introduction

This work is the first comprehensive analysis of the Czech migration to the United States, looking at both sides of the migration equation. No previous students of Czech migration to the United States in the nineteenth century used primary sources from both the departing and the receiving country. After World War II, the Communist rulers who came to power in 1948 put scholarship in Czechoslovakia into an ideological straitjacket. The topic of migration was considered dangerous because the post-1948 political leaders associated emigration with political dissent (many writers, artists, and intellectuals voted with their feet in the years immediately before and after the Communist takeover). Furthermore, scholarly work on nineteenth-century emigration would have required authors to write objectively about the "enemy"—the United States. Thus, Czech historians who wished to do research on the history of Czech emigration to the United States had no choice but to focus on the Czech-American urban "proletariat"—any other topic was politically taboo.

This analysis attempts to go beyond existing works, to shed new light on Czech migration abroad, and to take an objective look at the transitional experience of Czechs who decided to leave their homeland.

Useful generalizations about migration

From the dawn of European civilization, population movements have played a major role in shaping the history of the Western world. Europe's mass migrations in the second half of the nineteenth century were a by-product of sweeping social change on the continent. Many small landowners, cottagers, peasants, and agricultural laborers could not cope with the dislocations caused by the Industrial Revolution. Millions of Europeans chose the escape route across the Atlantic.

When we think of migration in the nineteenth century, we mistakenly assume only a transatlantic migration from Europe to America (from the Old World to the New World). To understand the phenomenon of migration, and to understand the immensity of the decision to migrate, we need to see the United States as only one—

albeit powerful—of the magnets on this planet. There were Europeans who had no desire to move to the United States. French, Spanish, Hungarians, and Finns, for example, migrated to the United States in small numbers. Many migrants were satisfied to move within Europe; many others went to the United States and then returned, only to re-emigrate later. Many Dutch who did not stay at home, for example, did not move to the United States—instead they migrated within the European continent.

Studies have shown that reasons for migration are complex and vary over time: political and religious oppression, economic depression, and a broad spectrum of personal reasons, or a mixture of all these factors—to name the main causes—motivated people's departure.

Perceptions of their own situations varied greatly among potential migrants: some people were born movers and some born stayers. Often, people with leadership qualities were the first ones to leave. The poorest peasants did not emigrate, at least not in the 1860s. The price of a ship ticket was too expensive for them. Although migrants are the focus of this analysis, the reaction of the society that stayed behind is also a part of the larger picture.[1]

With the exception of Irish emigration, most migrations were not caused by massive unbearable situations at home. Following the potato blight in 1848, the Irish had no choice but to emigrate. For them, the decision to emigrate or to stay was a matter of life or death (to stay was to die, to emigrate was to survive).

Germans, for instance, migrated in massive numbers, both within Europe and across the Atlantic. They went to the United States not so much to build something new as to preserve a way of life which seemed in danger of destruction in the new Europe. They travelled many thousands of miles for the sake of keeping their roots, customs, and family cohesion, and to remain the masters of their own destiny.[2] Most German migrants were not the poorest but the most intelligent and skilled (and thus relatively well-off) who had the self-confidence, wherewithal, and information to undertake the passage.

In sum, people left an environment of changing social and economic circumstances. Faced with these impersonal forces of historical magnitude, individuals were powerless to resist.

Czech migration

Within the wave of immigrants from Europe to the United States were emigrants from Bohemia and Moravia (Czechs and Moravians) who left in large numbers between 1860 and 1900, many of whom settled in the Midwest.* Nebraska, in particular, had a high concentration of Czech farmers, second only to Illinois (in 1910 Nebraska had 50,680 immigrants whose mother tongue was Czech).[3]

Generally, Czechs emigrated because they wanted to farm a large piece of land. They also wanted to secure a better future for their children, as this excerpt, written by a Czech pioneer in Minnesota, shows:

> We lack nothing now and are looking for a better future. But ... to bring virgin soil, for ages untouched, to its first harvest gives one hard calluses, and much perspiration flows over one's brow before he can enjoy its produce. Indeed, it was a bitter moment when I arrived at this, my purchased corner, with my whole family and there was nothing here but grass, shrubbery, and woods burned by Indians. That was our property, and that was the first calamity. As for the women, they have it worse—almost unbearable—in such situation. They like their comforts, and enjoy gossiping at coffee, but when they must bear any misfortune here, they do it without lamentations. And so we also endured before we put our buildings ... in these circumstances the immigrant who lacks enough industrious hands, a firm will and intrepid determination will come to no good end ... (not) everyone who comes here will be fortunate ... is everyone in Bohemia lucky? ... *whoever immigrates to America makes his lot worse, for he sacrifices himself that his descendants may fare better.* For these most of all, as you know, we immigrated here.[4] (italics mine)

---

*AUTHOR NOTE: The modern country of Czechoslovakia consisted until December 31, 1992, of four main parts: Bohemia, Silesia, Moravia (the Czech crown lands), and Slovakia. After January 1, 1993, the country was divided between the Czech Republic consisting of Bohemia, Moravia, Czech Silesia, and the new Republic of Slovakia occupying the territory of the traditional Slovak lands. Bohemians and Moravians came from the Czech lands. Only a small number of Slovaks settled west of the Mississippi River. This work, therefore, focuses only on the emigrants from Bohemia and Moravia.

Patterns of settlement

The first wave of Czech emigration, starting in the 1850s, went to New York City, St. Louis, Chicago, Milwaukee, and Texas. One decade later the second wave settled in Illinois and the upper Mississippi valley.

In the 1880s and 1890s, the only cities that continued to attract Czech immigrants were Chicago, Cleveland, and Omaha. Rural Iowa, Kansas, Oklahoma, California, and Nebraska became the new magnets.

A thorough analysis of the backgrounds of around 2,000 Czechs in Nebraska permitted the author to delineate the boundaries of the region in Bohemia-Moravia which had been swept by emigration fever—a wide belt stretching from southwestern Bohemia to eastern Moravia. More specifically, emigration swept the following regions of Bohemia: the south (to Vienna), the north (to Germany), and the center from the towns of Domažlice to Plzeň across to the mountains of the Šumava, to the Písek vicinity and on to the Tábor vicinity, and continuing on to the western side of the Czech-Moravian Highlands. Despite some differences in the geographical character of this belt, village-based agriculture was the common denominator.

Getting started on the American frontier was daunting, and Czech settlers often experienced pangs of insecurity.[5] As an ethnic group they settled close to each other in order to create a support network and perpetuate the folkways of the Old Country. They cherished their language and preserved it through cultural activities (for example, by putting on plays in the mother tongue). They organized dances and picnics. They also belonged to fraternal lodges that gave them material security and a sense of community, which was important to them.

As agricultural producers, Czechs were quite successful, adapting to the extent necessary to cope with new conditions. In social, religious, and cultural realms, however, this acculturation process was slower. Circumstances did not force Czechs to change their life, except in the economic realm. In farming, old methods gave way to an efficient and profitable mode of production, while in the spiritual life in its broadest sense "Czech" characteristics were retained much longer.

Politics and migration: 1848–1948

In 1848 politics and migration were two sides of the same coin—many intellectuals left in the aftermath of the 1848 revolution, when rising liberal and nationalistic aspirations were suppressed by the conservative Austrian monarchy. The monarchs of Europe were determined to prevent the ideas associated with the rise of Napoleonic France (and the youthful United States of America) from undermining the established order. In 1918, the new sovereign state of "Czechoslovakia" (effected by a merger of Bohemia, Moravia, and a part of Silesia with Slovakia) came into being after the military defeat and disintegration of the Austro-Hungarian Empire in World War I. The democratic republic, under the leadership of Tomáš G. Masaryk, a former professor of philosophy at Charles University, lasted until March 1939 when the Czech lands became a protectorate of Hitler's Third Reich, and Slovakia declared itself autonomous. Many people went into political exile after 1939, including the leaders of the Czech government.

In 1945, Czechoslovakia was reborn, thanks to the Allied armies. What is often most difficult for Americans to understand is how the Czech Communists could have emerged as the strongest party following the war. The reason is quite simple: it was the Communists who led the anti-Nazi resistance—in Czechoslovakia as elsewhere in Eastern Europe. In addition, the allied forces including the army of the Soviet Union liberated the country.

Stalin's foreign policy of territorial aggrandizement in Eastern Europe (aimed mainly at creating a buffer zone against future invasion) and the internal polarization of the political forces in Czechoslovakia led to a backlash of popular mistrust against the Communists. To forestall an electoral defeat which would have consigned them to the sidelines indefinitely, the Communists, no doubt with Stalin's blessing, staged a coup in February, 1948.

Politics and migration: the Communist era

For the second time in a single decade (1939–1948), the Dark Ages descended on Czechoslovakia. Innocent people were arrested on trumped-up charges, mock trials resulted in the imprisonment (or even execution) of opposition politicians and ordinary people. In the early 1950s, taking a cue from the Kremlin, the Communist party purged its own ranks of "untrustworthy" members. It was a terrifying time, when a knock on the door in the middle of the night could be the beginning of the end. A time when no one was safe, not even one's erstwhile tormentors: the Slánský show trials led to the execution of top-ranking Communist party officials. A time to get out if there was any way out. Scientists, writers, artists, athletes, and many others escaped because they could no longer express themselves freely.

In the 1960s, after "the thaw" in the Soviet Union which had been signalled by Nikita Khrushchev's Secret Speech at the 20th Party Congress in 1956 (when he denounced the "crimes of Stalin"), people in the East European states, including Czechoslovakia, could breathe more freely. Under the leadership of Antonín Novotný, the government eased travel restrictions and lifted its absolute ban on travel to Western Europe and the United States. As a result, fewer people felt the need to emigrate. Getting permission to travel abroad in the 1960s was not easy, but it was possible.

An attempt at political and economic reform of communism by reform-minded Communists culminated in January 1968 when Alexander Dubček, a Slovak, became the general secretary of the Communist Party. Dubček launched a liberalization campaign he called "socialism with a human face." He wanted to replace the ossified Communist dictatorship with a multiparty system responsive to the people. The Czechoslovak people welcomed this breath of fresh air, but hard-line leaders in Moscow and Prague thought Dubček's reforms would take Czechoslovakia out of the "socialist camp" (that is, the Warsaw Pact) and into the welcoming arms of the West. Nonetheless, the "Prague Spring" lasted seven and a half months. Then, on August 21, the armies of the Soviet Union and the other Warsaw Pact countries invaded a defenseless Czechoslovakia, thus bringing the dalliance with democracy to a tragic end. Leonid Brezhnev, the leader of the Soviet Union, declared that Moscow and its socialist allies had a right and duty to intervene in the internal affairs of other socialist states to preserve Soviet-style socialism. This assertion became the infamous Brezhnev Doctrine.

Purges of Dubček and other reform-minded Communists by the hard-liners ensued. People had tasted freedom and many Czechoslovaks, both young and old, were now bitterly disappointed and disillusioned. Emigration again rose dramatically. The majority who stayed in Czechoslovakia had no choice but to accommodate to the new regime and get on with their lives.

After the "normalization"—a euphemism for the purging and punishment of all opposition elements—only a few dissidents remained to carry on the struggle against the government. They circulated illegal works, and organized demonstrations on anniversaries commemorating important events in the country's history. They were often arrested and imprisoned. Václav Havel, the soft-spoken playwright who led the popular uprising that ousted the Communists in 1989, was to become not only Czechoslovakia's most famous dissident but also the conscience of the nation.

But Havel could not have succeeded were it not for the warm political winds blowing out of the Soviet Union after Mikhail Gorbachev launched his own Dubček-style liberalization movement in the mid-1980s. It was Gorbachev who set the stage for the collapse of Communism in Eastern Europe by rescinding the Brezhnev Doctrine. Youths celebrating Students' Day on November 17, 1989, marched through the streets of Prague, where they were met by armed police. Violent clashes occurred between government security forces and the students. Fortunately, no one was killed, but the police brutality prompted a public outrage. The result was the Velvet Revolution (so named because the revolution was remarkably non-violent). Václav Havel had been in prison at the beginning of 1989; in December, when the Communist government resigned, he became Czechoslovakia's new president—the first popular leader to govern the nation in over four decades. Since 1989, many emigres who left after 1948 and again after 1968 returned. Having left for political reasons, they now came back for political reasons. History had come full circle and, for these refugees from tyranny, a long, dark night had finally ended.

Hark the River Niobrara,
How lively it is along your shores,
and the meadows around are so pretty,
Tired heart is rejuvenated by you
Bohemia found here a new home
having left the country of his birth
Those who are looking for wealth
must follow a thorny path!
He runs along with a plow
and this is an honor for every Bohemian.
He wants to race through the deserted
    prairie
to reap a bountiful harvest.
What about you fish in the stream?
you are mine with such an ease. . .

I am breathing freedom,
and the stream bubbles in the quiet country
But my heart so often aches
It yearns for my homeland
The ache is like a needle piercing through it
Any pleasure will not replace my dear
    motherland!

This poem, "Pleasure and Pain," written in 1874 by Josef Šedivý, one of the founding members of the Niobrara Czech settlement in Knox County, speaks to the odd mixture of awe and desolation that many early Czech immigrants in Nebraska experienced.

AUTHOR NOTE: Josef Šedivý, "Slasti a Bol," *Pokrok Západu* (24 March 1874): 4.

Part I

Out of the Old World

Chapter 1

 Background of
Emigration in Bohemia

The emigration from the Czech lands to the United States began in the 1840s and reached its peak in the 1880s and 1890s. Several students of migratory processes have suggested that to understand the complex phenomena of migration and to explain the behavior of "hyphenated" Americans, one needs to follow settlers, in the words of Brigitte Ogden, "from their places of birth to their place of death."[1] The "classical" conditions that were part of the complex picture that gave rise to the great exodus of Czechs to America between the 1860s and 1880s were generally associated with the disruptive effects of modernization and mechanization on the traditional patterns of life and work in rural Czech society.

The setting: Czech lands in transition

Emigrants left Bohemia and Moravia at a time when this region was becoming the industrial base of the Austro-Hungarian Empire: by the end of the nineteenth century the Czech lands boasted a developed agri-industrial economy on a par with the most developed countries in the world.[2] For example, in the 1860s this region employed 60 percent of the industrial workforce in the Austrian Empire. Indeed, the pace of industrialization in the Czech lands was comparable to that of France, and was close to that of Germany.[3] Why did Czechs leave a country that was undergoing rapid economic growth? And why were some areas within Bohemia-Moravia more emigration prone than others?

Area covered by the Austro-Hungarian Empire. 1867–1918.

Economic growth and population explosion have long been discarded as the sole reasons for emigration. The factors influencing the decision to emigrate are complex, and the intensity of any one or combination of factors varies greatly from case to case. Within the large set of "push" factors there existed both general and individual reasons that brought people to the decision to leave. We shall look first at the general factors.

Socio-economic stratification

Broad patterns of social and economic change are often more complicated than they appear to be on the surface. The role of the social historian is to sort out the evidence beneath the surface and assemble it, like the pieces of a jigsaw puzzle, in a way that most closely fits the realities of a past which has long since faded from memory.

The Industrial Revolution affected different parts of rural Bohemia-Moravia quite differently. The fertile areas in eastern

Bohemia along the river Elbe could withstand the fluctuation of cereals prices; the peasants in this prosperous agricultural region fared well. Thanks to bountiful harvests in this region, Bohemia and Moravia were the main producers of grain in Austria.[4] In places where land ownership was highly concentrated, the dislocations accompanying the Industrial Revolution polarized the rural society, as large "agribusinesses" dictated domestic prices which were increasingly linked to competitive world-market prices. The falling price of agricultural commodities split Czech farmers into a large underclass of poor peasants living at a subsistence level and having to supplement their income as day laborers, on one hand, and a small group of large landowners dominating the market, mechanizing to some extent, and gradually organizing their farms into rudimentary agro-industries, on the other.

Many poor peasants were forced to give up their small plots and seek employment on the large estates. Frequently, they had to "moonlight" by engaging in crafts or working part-time in construction. Full-time farm work was not always easy to find, as some rich landowners looked to machines rather than hired hands for help.[5]

Thus agriculture followed the same path as textiles and other industries (albeit somewhat more slowly)—the most efficient mode of production was to be found on the large estates, whose owners had sufficient capital to invest in modern technology. These innovative farm operators dominated the market and gradually forced out many small and relatively inefficient producers.

A lower class, one step higher than the landless underclass on the socio-economic ladder, also emerged. It comprised the numerous agricultural producers who tilled land (either owned or rented) not exceeding five acres. These small farmsteads were too tiny to support a family, which meant that family members had to work for other farmers to supplement the family income. As agricultural producers, they contributed little to the marketplace, consuming most of what they grew.

Above the lower class were two intermediate classes: the cottager (*malorolník*) and the farmer (*střední rolník* or *sedlák*). The first group owned ten to twelve acres of land, had skills, and the more wealthy cottagers could afford to hire laborers. Unlike those in the class immediately below them, most cottagers produced for the grain market.

The *sedlák* was the symbol of the Czech village, although these individuals made up a relatively small but confident group that was slowly forming into a rural bourgeoisie. Their landholdings were extremely modest by American standards. They owned between twelve and fifty acres of land, usually had a modest additional income from an enterprise in the village such as a workshop, wanted to be economically independent, used hired workers, and grew most of the produce for the market. The *sedlák* was the symbol of the successful peasant, a romantic figure representing a way of life that was fading into the past, the embodiment of an idyllic existence which many rural Czechs felt powerless to preserve. The emergence of a national agricultural economy threatened even the relatively prosperous *sedlák* because he could not compete with the largest landowners who increasingly dominated the market. Already in the waning years of the nineteenth century, the "get big or get out" principle was taking its toll on the smallholder.

The large landowners—German-speaking squires—were numerically a small, internally stratified group. In general, they owned more than fifty acres of land, but the richest group in this category were aristocrats whose landholdings typically exceeded 250 acres and who also had industrial and banking interests.

The transformation from labor- to capital-intensive farming was not a smooth process, as old traditions and customs stood in the way of efficiency. Mechanized methods of production called for fewer employees in agriculture. The most modern-minded farmers realized that it was necessary to mechanize in order to survive. Nature played a role too: farmers in flat regions—for example, along the river Elbe—were at an advantage in comparison with farmers from the hills because they could more easily use machinery.[6]

Ironically, the emancipation of the serfs in 1848 created an incentive to mechanize (and thus push smallholders off the farm). After 1848, the sudden, short-term shortage of labor caused large landowners to turn to technology out of necessity.[7] By the 1870s and 1880s, Czech industry was producing farm machinery (prior to this time Czech farmers had to import such implements from England). Further advances in mechanization came in the 1890s, when better ploughs, mowers, and threshing machines were introduced. The mechanization of Czech agriculture shortened the period of time needed for labor-intensive work such as sowing and thrashing. Also, the first chemical fertilizers date from this period—another sign of the times.

The use of machinery, however, can easily be overstated; by the end of the nineteenth century Czech agriculture was still far from being fully mechanized.[8] One of the characteristic by-products of the transformation in agriculture was the use of hired laborers. In the medium-sized farmsteads—twelve to twenty-five acres—at least one-third of the farmers used hired workers; farmers with fifty to one hundred acres were even more likely to use such workers. All farms larger than 100 acres used them. Small farmers, on the other hand, could not afford to pay hired workers. With the exception of specialized agricultural units such as gardening, vegetable growing, or hops growing farms, employment of a non-relative by a farmer who owned less than twelve acres of land was rare.[9]

The folowing table, which gives the yields for key crops in 1880–1892, suggests that much of Czech agriculture was still tied to traditional modes of production.[10]

Grain production on Czech lands—1880–1892 (in bushels/acre)				
wheat	rye	barley	oats	potatoes
20.3	18.2	20.4	30.6	102.8

Source: Otto Urban, *Československé dějiny, 1848–1914*, 57.

Most small (up to five acres) and medium (five to twelve acres) farmsteads used human power. If owners of these estates had a cow they used it for both its pulling power and also for dairy purposes. The owners of medium to large estates (twelve to fifty acres) usually had horses. (Only one percent of small farms and four percent of middle-sized farms had a horse.) Most (75 percent) of the landowners of estates larger than fifty acres had at least one horse.[11]

By the early twentieth century nearly all the large estates were mechanized, but only one-fifth of the small farms used farming machinery. The large landowners drove small farmers out of business, forcing them to sell or face foreclosure. The dispossessed became hired hands or left the village.

The size of one's landholding was a significant indicator of economic success, but the relationship was a complex one—local conditions such as soil quality and cropping patterns were important, too. Data from 1896 showed that more than half of the land of even large estates (fifty acres and more) was still covered by forests.[12]

What were the consequences of this growing socio-economic stratification of Czech agriculture? A large estate owner or a successful farmer with more than fifty acres sold almost ninety percent of his production. Peasants who owned land not exceeding twelve acres usually came to the market with approximately one-half of their produce.

Peasants either adjusted to the conditions at home or left in search of a better livelihood. According to contemporary estimates, a peasant family with less than five acres of land consumed twenty times less than the family living on a large estate exceeding two hundred acres.[13] Most farms were at least twenty-five acres in size, but farmers could live on plots as little as five acres if they specialized in horticulture, i.e., growing vegetables and planting fruit trees.[14]

At the turn of the century one-third of all the peasants worked on land that was wholly or partially rented.[15] This situation reflected the increasing concentration of land ownership in Bohemia-Moravia. Poor farmers usually rented out of necessity, whereas rich farmers rented to get richer. The smallest and largest operators were the most common renters. Peasants in the middle were least likely to rent, probably because they had neither the need nor the means (money and machinery) to do so.[16]

Most peasants could not avoid having to borrow money. But credit was difficult to obtain, and loan terms favored the financiers. Land-owning aristocrats had a direct interest in the nascent banking system, which meant that debtors who could not repay their loans stood to lose their land to the banks. Foreclosure became one of the mechanisms by which land was being consolidated and concentrated.

Owners of small plots of land were the main debtors. Sixty to seventy percent of small farms (twelve acres or less) were in debt. Foreclosures were most common in this category.[17] There was probably a fine line between a sale and a foreclosure because many impoverished peasants very likely sold their land under duress, i.e., sell it today or lose it tomorrow.

On December 21, 1867, the monarchy promulgated a civil rights law (no. 142/1867). This law included a broad grant of civil liberties, including property rights. Thereafter, the sale of land rose rapidly. Between 1868 and 1887 one-tenth of all agricultural land in Bohemia-Moravia changed hands. Three-quarters of this land was sold on the market and the rest was transferred through inheritance or foreclosure.[18]

Paradoxically, while much of the land was being concentrated into larger holdings, the number of farms actually grew by thirty percent between 1860 and 1890, due to a parallel process of parcelling. These two contradictory trends—consolidation and fragmentation of landholding—affected exclusively the smallest and the largest farmsteads, indicating the gradual demise of the middling peasants who as a class were among the biggest losers to modernization.[19] The number of smallholdings (twelve acres or less) increased during this period by approximately 90 percent. The number and the total acreage of medium-sized holdings decreased. The acreage of the smallest and the largest holdings grew.[20]

Regionalism was an important factor in these changes. Four main economic regions emerged during the gestation period of the Industrial Revolution in the second half of the nineteenth century: the region with traditional textile production, the new industrial region, the fertile agricultural region with intensive forms of cash-crop production and a food-processing industry growing up along-side it, and the infertile region with no industries.[21]

The last category (the poorest regions), characteristically swept by the emigration fever, covered more than one-third of the Czech lands and was the largest of all. Southwest Bohemia, northwestern and southeastern portions of the Bohemian Forest, the mid-portion of southern Bohemia, the České Budějovice region, the Třeboň region, an area immediately east of Prague, the central and the southern parts of the Czech-Moravian Highlands, and the Znojmo region had no industrial base to balance off the economic deficit caused by the low agricultural productivity.[22] This geographic area was not homogeneously poor, of course; there were pockets of prosperity in a landscape of economic stagnation.

Population transitions

Population pressure combined with economic frustration was another factor at play in the emigration-prone areas. The population of the Czech lands grew by nearly 45 percent in the second half of the nineteenth century, from 6.6 million in 1846 to more than 10 million in 1910.[23] According to demographer Ludmila Kárníková, "From the second half of the 18th century up until the First World War the Czech lands went through a period of stormy evolution."[24]

The migration within the empire from rural areas to the cities brought about a demographic transformation during this period.[25] Regions with outmoded industry or inefficient agriculture suffered depopulation, while new industrial centers grew rapidly.[26] The coal-mining regions and the market and transportation hubs such as the areas around Praha, Brno, Ostrava, and Plzeň were the magnets that drew the displaced peasants and landless laborers from the villages to the cities.[27]

While Czech industry benefited from free trade, agricultural producers looked to the government for protective measures against cheap American wheat.[28] Czech farmers from the less fertile regions began to see the handwriting on the wall and started leaving villages for towns, industrial regions, or other countries.[29]

The exodus from the villages, which began in 1850, affected only certain areas. The agricultural crisis of the 1870s—a crisis induced by competition from foreign (mainly American) producers—intensified the rates of emigration. The climax came in the 1880s when over 17,000 people left Austria-Hungary (most of whom were probably Bohemians and Moravians), as the flooding of Europe by cheap American wheat drove many Czech farmers to the brink of destitution. Ironically, then, it was American agriculture that spurred many Czech farmers to depart for the United States.[30]

Generally speaking, industrial centers experienced the highest population growth rates. On the other hand, only in a few rural areas, such as the valleys of southern Moravia and the fertile strip along the river Elbe did the population not decline.[31] These two areas, specializing in certain cash crops, weathered the agricultural crisis of the 1880s without depopulation due to urbanization and emigration.[32]

Opportunities in towns fluctuated with the changing fortunes of industry, which in turned affected the rate and the direction of emigration from Czech lands.[33] Czechs departing from Bohemia-Moravia in the 1860s and 1870s went to Lower Austria, particularly to Vienna, and to the United States. Some also went to Russia and Germany.[34]

After the turn of the century the agricultural situation improved; following a short crisis when wheat prices fell in the mid-1890s, prices began to rise. By increasing the tariff on wheat and adopting other protective measures, the government was able to stem the tide of emigration.[35]

Chapter 2

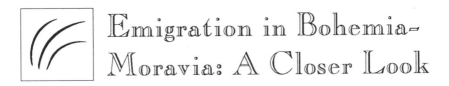 Emigration in Bohemia-
Moravia: A Closer Look

For people who have never gone more than a few miles from where they were born, emigration is an extreme act—perhaps even an act of desperation. The life and times of the simple peasants who emigrated from the Czech lands in the 1870s is something distant and abstract for Americans living in the twilight of the twentieth century; but the problems these peasants faced, the fears and frustrations that drove them to take what must have seemed like a leap into the abyss, were all too real.

This chapter focuses on a single area in a region of the country from which many people emigrated after 1870. An in-depth study of one region is perhaps the best way to get a feel for the way things were, to recapture a sense of the times, and to gain insights into the nature of Czech peasant life—into the kind of world Czech immigrants left behind. It is to be expected that the personality and character of immigrants who settled in the Midwest were molded by the culture and society from which they sprang.

The context of Czech emigration

Emigration started in the 1850s but affected only certain areas in Bohemia-Moravia, occurring at different times, and with varying degrees of intensity. The climax came in the 1880s when over 17,000 people came from Austria-Hungary, most of whom were Bohemians and Moravians.[1]

Through the examination of the places of origin of Nebraska-Czechs, and of city directories of New York, St. Louis, Cleveland, and Chicago, it is possible to draw boundaries delineating the emigration landscape starting in southwest Bohemia, making a swing around southern Bohemia, and extending to the Czech-Moravian Highlands west of Brno, the largest Moravian city. There was also an area forty-five miles east of Prague, the Kutná Hora region, which produced a significant number of emigrants.

By the standards of economic and physical geography, the major Czech emigration zones are heterogeneous, so that certain characteristics apply to certain districts and not to others. Local factors and conditions played an important role as causes of emigration. Even so, a few generalizations are in order.

The region in question is hilly with fields and meadows rarely spoiled by smokestacks and other imprints of industrialization. Most of the country appears to be a place where time stood still. In short, the region people left was a backwater, described by one writer as an "infertile farming land with no industry."[2]

The Czech and Slovak lands (Bohemia, Moravia, Lower Silesia, and Slovakia) formed Czechoslovakia in 1918. In January of 1993 the country divided into the The Czech Republic (Bohemia, Moravia, and Lower Silesia), and The Slovak Republic (Slovakia).

A high-impact area: the Czech-Moravian Highlands

A statistical analysis of the data on Nebraska's Czech settlers in the last two decades of the nineteenth century reveals that an overwhelming majority of immigrants came from the foothills of the Czech-Moravian Highlands. These emigrants were probably the last major wave of Czechs from the Austro-Hungarian Empire.

The reasons for leaving were varied, but social and economic changes seem to be particularly pronounced. A paucity of capital, a shortage of water, and an unenterprising spirit were deficiencies common throughout the region. During the recurring economic crises that began in the 1870s work-for-wages became increasingly scarce.

The technological changes of the nineteenth century wiped out the small industries. The beginnings of the Industrial Revolution bypassed the region,[3] and the strength of the feudal guild system was a deterrent to forces of change.[4] As a result of the mechanization of the old textile areas of northern Bohemia, the weaver's trade, once the Czech-Moravian Highlands' most important industry, was in decline. The production of starch for a time filled in the gap, after a few enterprising individuals started a cottage starch industry in Polná in 1850.[5] The farmers in the vicinity of the towns of Polná, Německý Brod, and Přibyslav, grew potatoes and supplied the towns that manufactured starch.[6] Poor potato harvests and price competition eventually defeated this nascent industry.

Only a few industries, all employing small numbers of workers, existed in the cities. Jihlava, the hub of the region, had a cotton factory built in the eighteenth century, a brewery, a sugar factory, tannery, and a small-scale production of mustard, vinegar, fats and oils, and chicory.[7] Most of the industries were dependent on agriculture production in the region but employed few laborers.[8] (A distillery in Hrotovice, for example, employed forty workers.)[9] Thus the region's industry could not siphon off the surplus rural population that had to remain in rural areas and survive on tiny plots of land or try to find work on large estates.

The lack of raw materials, good roads, and railroads in this area was an added barrier standing in the way of the industrialization that was in progress in most of the Czech lands.[10] The railroad network designed during the first half of the nineteenth century missed the whole region. The poor-quality roads could not make up for the lack of railroads.[11]

Farming in this area required a greater investment than, for example, in Eastern Bohemia around the river Elbe. (The region along the banks of the Elbe is blessed with fertile soil which supported the local peasants rather comfortably; not surprisingly, only few left the area in search of a better livelihood.) Two-thirds of the land in the Žďár nad Sázavou and the Jihlava region is arable but the quality of soil is poor, shallow and infertile, and the land has to be plowed three to four times a year.[12]

The unfavorable soil conditions made intensive farming necessary. Under such circumstances, most peasants diversified in order to sustain themselves and perhaps have some produce for the market. In other words, they grew vegetables as well as cereals. According to the geographical classification, the soil was most suitable for wheat and potatoes.[13]

The climate is also unfavorable for farming, with long winters and a short growing season. In most of the area the average temperature is about 46 degrees Fahrenheit.[14] Strong cold winds come in spring with frequent frosts. Hail is common and heavy rain often erodes the soil which is otherwise quite dry. In the nineteenth century one-fourth of the region needed an irrigation system and crop rotation.[15]

The main crops were wheat, oats, rye, legumes, potatoes, chicory, hemp, and fodder.[16] Flax was a profitable crop for a time; with the decline of weaver's trade, however, flax growing all but disappeared by 1900. Specialization in one crop often ended in a disaster; still, some peasants took the risk and grew only potatoes. Following the bad potato harvest of 1881 in Bohemia, many peasants became destitute, took what belongings they could, and left without even selling the piece of ground they owned.[17]

Several parts of the region specialized in fruit growing. There were plum and cherry orchards in almost every village, and fruit trees lined roads and paths—a pattern still visible throughout much of this region.[18] In the gardens protected by a fence from animals, people grew cabbage and other vegetables for sale. Farmers raised horses, cattle, and swine.[19]

Most of the landholdings were small in this part of the country. As a consequence of the liberal law of 1867, which allowed landowners to dispose of land at will, parents unable to buy more land parcelled the small piece of land they had, dividing little "handkerchief plots" among their children or selling them to landless peasants. This practice, in time, made farming highly inefficient.[20] It is noteworthy that stringent inheritance laws caused sons and daughters in some European countries to emigrate, and that the liberal inheritance laws of the Austro-Hungarian Empire produced the same result—a rural exodus—though for different reasons. It was especially the young people who left because parcellization meant that most children could hope to inherit no more than a small fragment of land insufficient to support a family.[21]

The cottagers, unable to run a large-size agricultural enterprise that would require mechanization and modern technology, struggled in vain against the threat of loss of land due to insolvency, a common "disease." Each member of a peasant family had to work the land to make ends meet. If a father wanted to send his children to high school he often had to sell part of his property. [22]

In an effort to survive, the cottagers braided brooms and mats, repaired shoes in the winter, or worked in the forests. The second income helped to sustain the family but was not enough to modernize, to buy new equipment, or to purchase more lands.[23]

Although small plots of land dotted the countryside, there were a few large estate owners who typically owned the best land.[24] These estates expanded as their owners bought up the smaller landholdings of financially hard-pressed peasants.[25] For example, in Těchobuz in the Pacov district, one landlord owned 56.48 percent of all available land.[26] Such estate owners either rented out the land at high rates or hired laborers.[27]

The new serfs: the *čeledín* and *děvečka*

Due to the small numbers of large landowners only a few people could work as hired hands. A hired laborer (*čeledín*) or a hired maid (*děvečka*) could also be too young to own a piece of land. The *čeledín*, once hired, was at his employer's mercy. The nature of the relationship is evident from a law signed by the Austrian Emperor in 1866 requiring all hired hands to carry a special document (*čeledínská knížka*) similar to an internal passport.

A *čeledínská knížka* was a kind of a contract between the master/ farmer and the *čeledín*. The passport/contract was also an identity card with descriptive data such as age, height, weight, and hair color, and the *čeledín* was obligated to carry it with him.[28] Without this document the person was automatically suspect, and a farmer was liable for a fine if he hired a person without one. The regulations of employment were strict. The *čeledín* was sentenced to a fine or a prison sentence if found guilty of anything forbidden by the contract. A sample from one such contract (translated by the author) reads as follows:

> A hired hand has to be obedient and faithful to the farmer, he has to show respect, speak the truth, he needs to work hard ... If he is hired for certain services and is subsequently asked to perform additional services he needs to comply with the wishes of the lord ... He could be asked to perform services in the field although originally he might not have been hired for such services.[29]

The contractual rules were strict regarding the obligations of the *čeledín* but the obligations of the lord to the *čeledín* were vague. Fees had to be exchanged between the laborer and the estate owner to ensure a mutual commitment. The lord gave the hired hand room and board and paid him a small wage. The *čeledín* could leave only under certain specific circumstances. When the lord dismissed the worker, no law could force him to accept the *čeledín* back but arrangements were supposed to be made regarding the loss of board and wages to the *čeledín*, according to the language of the contract.[30]

The hired laborers slept in small chambers or in barns next to horses. They ate with the master's family. Estate owners decided if and when the *čeledín* could leave the house or receive visitors. The *čeledín* was obliged to report any dishonest act by fellow laborers to the master; a *čeledín* who failed to do so was punished. The *čeledín* had to keep all his belongings inside a trunk in the house. When the contract expired the lord checked the belongings of the *čeledín*.

The *čeledín* had to serve his master for a minimum of one year. Counting the many state and religious holidays together with Sundays, hired laborers in theory had one hundred days off a year! In practice, however, the *čeledín* and *děvečka* worked on holidays and Sundays if asked. In addition to doing field work at planting and harvest times, the *čeledín* looked after animals and worked around the house.

The annual wage of the *čeledín* was sixty to seventy florins ($160–190), which included room and board. The farmer paid out wages in four increments, the highest after the months of July, August, and September. Farm hands looking after animals received thirty-five to forty-five florins, and a maid thirty to forty. Some laborers received payment in cloth or the use of a plot of land to grow flax. Women were typically paid less than men.[31] A *čeledín* could in principle become a landowner, an eventuality which was explicitly mentioned in the *čeledínská knížka*.[32]

The master could dismiss a hired laborer at any time. The *čeledín* could also break the contract if he was abused or if his life was endangered. If the estate owner disputed the charges, however, the lord mayor of the nearest town acted as the arbiter; in most cases the mayor favored the employer.

Contemporary accounts suggest that people in villages complained about the work ethic and morals of the *čeledín*, believing such a person to be unreliable, disloyal, and lazy, according to a survey taken at the end of the last century.[33] The life of the *čeledín* was said to be carefree and happy. The impression one gets from a survey taken at the time is that these latter-day indentured servants spent most of their time eating, drinking, making merry, and dancing the polka. In all probability, this picture is overdrawn—the life of the hired hand was far from idyllic and if he (she) drank and danced on occasion it was most likely to escape from the drab and dreary reality of everyday life.

When an estate owner ran out of patience with his hired hand, the *čeledín* had to go in search of other employment. Those who could not find work locally migrated seasonally to Austria and worked there during the harvest seasons, and in sugar factories.[34] Many decided to go overseas.

The struggle for survival

Land was expensive and scarce. Land shortage and land hunger combined to drive prices to unprecedented levels.[35] The threat of losing one's land was common to most cottagers and landowning peasants in general.

Judging from applications for permission to emigrate, the threat of sale due to insolvency was frequently stated as the reason for leaving. The evidence indicates, however, that the emigrants were not destitute, but left to avoid forced auctions or foreclosures and to avoid becoming paupers. By leaving before disaster struck, they kept control of their lives, exiting when they could still afford to pay for the passage. If the local farm prices were bad or the crops rotted, as was the case during the rainy year of 1881, many people left for the United States without even staying long enough to sell their land.[36] In general, only the death of an heirless owner resulted in a voluntary land sale. Auctions most frequently occurred under financial duress and were the smallholders' only option other than foreclosure.[37]

Many craftsmen left villages to go to the United States. Generally, having a skill helped, but the demand for services was limited in the villages. Lomeč (formerly Velký Lomeč), a village of about four hundred people that could support only one blacksmith and a shoemaker, was a case in point. Other local craftsmen in these trades had to find jobs elsewhere because they could not survive here. Some earned extra money as musicians or moonlighting in other ways.[38]

The *Anketa*: surveying the problem

The problems in the depressed regions became the target of a government investigation, ordered in 1876 by the Assembly of the Kingdom of Bohemia and published twenty years later under the name of *Anketa* (literally, "questionnaire").[39] Eighty-seven interviewers questioned farm producers and local government officials about the situation in agriculture.[40] In each of the fifty-six geographical survey areas, the interviewers asked questions about annual crop yields, emigration rates, the availability of insurance, the existence of producers' associations, ideas for innovations, quality of schools, and other related measures of socio-economic conditions.[41]

The results of the study confirmed the impact on the Czech lands of the economic crisis of the 1870s—a depression, really. In Bohemia-Moravia, the financial crisis of May 1873 brought down the prices of such products as sugar and grain alcohol.

Speculation contributed to falling grain prices as well.[42] But the worst problems facing the peasants were a cost-price squeeze (paying more for what they bought and getting less for what they sold), bad harvests or outright crop failures, difficulties in obtaining credit, and rising debt.[43]

The *Anketa* surveyors described how many farmers lived in what the surveyors considered to be an extravagant lifestyle.[44] If true, the debt crisis in Czech agriculture during this period was in large part self-inflicted. What seems more likely, however, is that forces beyond the control of the producers were at work undermining the viability of small farms in the last quarter of the nineteenth century.

Nevertheless, the producers were by no means free of responsibility for their own plight. Most farmers were slow to accept changes in farming techniques.[45] Resistance to modern technology resulted in an inadequate use of fertilizers and continued reliance on old-fashioned methods of cultivation. The few farmers who could afford to innovate were often reluctant to do so, because they did not understand or trust the new equipment and methods (much as some people today have an aversion to computers).

Every district had an agrarian society designed to educate farmers in new production techniques.[46] Many farmers were interested in educational programs, and agricultural magazines were available, but their impact was apparently quite limited.[47]

An adherence to the three-field system, in which two-thirds of the land was plowed and planted and the rest was left to lie fallow, was an old-fashioned method still prevalent in the Czech-Moravian Highlands and other poor regions. Peasants used the unsown land as pasture for cattle grazing. Alternate cropping—sowing different crops from one year to the next—only gradually replaced the three-field system.[48]

A great portion of the grain was lost in the fields because birds ate most of it before it could start to grow.[49] The large landowners used an expensive swing-plough; the poor sowed by hand. Smallholders worked with the old-fashioned simple wooden implements.[50] The more progressive peasants founded cooperatives and pooled resources for the purchase of expensive machinery. In the village of Lomeč, a hand-powered threshing machine was purchased in 1870 through a cooperative effort.[51]

Machines made farming easier for wealthy and progressive producers. Machines for the sowing of beet root and flax were available from the 1850s. A wealthy farmer had on an average two to five ploughs, harrows, and rollers, and at least three weeding machines.[52] He reaped the grain by scythe and thrashed it in a barn by flail. [53]

For a poor peasant farm animals were a luxury. In the absence of a horse and wagon, he would carry the manure on his back. Many who did have domestic animals did not take proper care of them, partly because children and teenagers were often given this task.[54] On an average, poor peasants had only one cow or, at most, two.[55] The government tried to remedy the situation in 1908 by supporting the cattle-poor districts with an emergency fund. The areas which qualified for such subsidies were also, not by accident, the main emigration regions.[56]

If the peasant could not afford a hired hand the whole family worked in the field. Women and children hoed, pulled the plough, and carried the harvest. No farm work was exclusively done by either women or men. The women, however, typically cut the wheat by sickle, while the men used scythes.[57] Peasants milled the flour in hand-powered home mills shortly before they would use it for baking because the grain kept longer than the flour.[58]

The workers sheaved the wheat and dried it in the fields, and then burned the stubble.[59] They thrashed the wheat with flails, and cleaned the grain by throwing it against the wind. Following the harvest, transportation to the consumer was a problem. The north-west railroad system charged high tariffs and the owners gave no discount rates to peasants.[60]

There were three main groups of peasants in regions such as the foothills of the Czech-Moravian Highlands. The first category included the near-destitute peasants with either no land or a small plot of land; the second numerically small category consisted of the rich farmers who controlled the market and, in effect, set the grain prices. The third was the middle group of farmers, who lived in constant danger of losing their land, livelihood, and social status. The peasants were helpless against these trends; understandably, they sought political representation, but to no avail.[61]

The "political" issues of importance to farm producers in the 1870s ran the gamut from substantial to ridiculous. For example, some farmers wanted to limit the number of dances in the villages because they perceived a connection between dances and children born out of wedlock. (It was quite common for hired hands to have illegitimate children.)[62] To cite another example, because farmers needed help with the harvest, many favored shortening the military service (in 1869 it was in fact shortened from seven to three years).[63] Farmers also demanded that military exercises should not be held during harvest season so as not to take youths away when they were most needed.[64]

Farmers looked to the government for help in other matters as well.[65] Taxation was a major concern. Farm producers paid two taxes, a property tax and a land tax; a system most farmers considered unfair, favoring a progressive tax on farm producers instead. The peasants further sought a protective tariff against the import of foreign grain and cattle, and also wanted debt relief, easier credit, and universal insurance in case of fire, hail, and illness.[66]Home insurance was common, but pension plans were unaffordable and the returns were small.[67]

Help came too late for many Czechs and Moravians.[68] The lack of heavy industry nearby forced peasants to travel great distances in search of work. Many tried their luck in Austria or Germany before they headed for Hamburg or Bremen, the two main points of embarkation for America.

Village life: what they left behind

Between 1870 and 1880 Czech emigration to Vienna and to the United States resulted in the serious depopulation of the Czech-Moravian Highlands and other poor agricultural regions.[69]

Emigrants from the Czech-Moravian Highlands left behind small villages of approximately two hundred people that dotted the countryside. Czech and Moravian settlements had a communal character. The number of houses in a rural settlement varied with the size of the population but there were usually about thirty houses for two hundred peasants and cottagers. A church or chapel and a two-story manor containing local administrative offices, a district court, and perhaps an inland revenue office, dominated the village. Often there was a large lake and a forested area in the back.

A justice of the peace or a magistrate and aldermen ran the village.[70] The Austrian government wanted to decentralize the empire in the 1860s. As a part of this process it redefined the role of a village by giving it administrative autonomy. Village aldermen became decision-makers in matters affecting local order, schools, public charity, and the village property and economy. The crown made everybody in the village legally entitled to a share in public affairs. The rich landowners and established farmers resented this dalliance with democracy because it meant they were not only losing their economic status to the forces of modernization, but also their social status to the lower class of cottagers and landless peasants with whom they now had to share power. The local elite struggled to retain control through an increase in local taxes and fees charged to the socially disadvantaged strata of the village population. The end result was that many wealthy farmers decided to go because having to share political power threatened their social position. Many poor peasants often chose to emigrate because they detested being treated as social inferiors and did not want to pay more taxes. The economic crises only deepened the dissatisfaction of both groups.[71]

The position of wealthy farmers within the village showed the social stratification of a rural settlement. Their houses, next to the church and the parish house, faced the village green, had "high, curved frames above entrances which were representative of Baroque Revival."[72] The stone or brick houses of the well-to-do farmers dominated the center of the village.

Houses of peasants stood next to one another in close proximity. Owners used oak or pine wood as building materials. They painted the buildings white and decorated them in either black, gray, or blue at the base. The window coves contained pictures of saints or little statuettes. Flower gardens decorated the front yards; the decorative facades of the houses faced the streets; barns and vegetable gardens were at the back of the houses. Wooden or brick cow sheds stood nearby.[73] The houses and gardens, with sheds and barns, were fenced in. The village green had a rectangular shape, often with a duck pond in the middle of it.[74]

Extended families lived together in rural settlements. The retired farmer (*výměnkář*) owned the house but lived in a smaller structure (*výměnek*) attached to the main farmhouse. He and his wife also had a vegetable garden. The *výměnkář* continued to help in the field but his son—the heir—was in charge of managing the farm operation. The heir of the farmstead or the house had to give to the *výměnkář* a set quantity of the crop and animals.[75]

In the Czech-Moravian Highlands rural settlements were self-contained units which the inhabitants rarely left. Most villages had a primary school; only towns had secondary schools, however.[76] A village might also have a town hall, a cemetery, and a parsonage.[77]

Traditional life in the villages only slowly gave way to the global trend of modernization. Ceremonial, communal, and family customs were an integral part of village life, reflecting economic conditions, social structure, legal principles, religious and moral ideals, and hygienic practices.[78] A durable tapestry of folkways and festivals formed the backdrop for a rich social life, not a life of isolation so common to American farmers. The world Czech immigrants left behind was not all bad; nor could many of the good things—especially the sense of community, of having roots in a place, of belonging—be taken with them.

The most festive occasion of all in the Czech-Moravian Highlands was a wedding. The wedding customs were merry and uninhibited. The ceremony of dressing up the bride was accompanied by much frivolity. The wedding lasted several days, starting in the afternoon of the day before the ceremony; on the day of the wedding there was much eating, drinking, and dancing.[79]

The wedding party sang to the accompaniment of instruments while marching to the church. The religious element had roots in secular customs.[80] A typical nineteenth-century wedding took place in a tavern, a place for social gatherings in most villages. All the ceremonial events in rural areas, including the celebrations of the different saints, had in common a feast accompanied by much drinking, loud music, singing, and dancing that lasted until the following morning.[81] A wedding, for example, was not merely a family affair, but a village affair in which everyone from the surrounding area participated.

Funerals were accompanied by traditions and superstitions symbolizing the deceased's return to the ground. People in villages accepted death as a normal part of the life cycle apart from any religious meaning. The deceased received an emotional farewell from relatives and neighbors.[82]

Annual celebrations were part of village traditions. The most important was a feast following the harvest that included dancing and drinking. The villagers had to contribute to this feast. Similar celebrations were held during the winter months, for which the villagers dressed up in costumes and usually took part in lively processions.[83]

The old communal traditions and bonds permeated into farming and the daily life. Neighbors helped each other in cases of a catastrophe or with building a house.[84] The importance of communal feeling explains people's propensity to organize into cooperatives and other associations such as fraternal lodges, *sokols* (gymnastic organizations), and patriotic clubs (*Slovanská lípa*), when they moved to the New World.[85] It also explains why many Czech immigrants complained of homesickness and a feeling of isolation in America.

Going to the village church on Sundays and to the village inn was a chance to dress up. In the nineteenth century people in most areas stopped wearing folk costumes and dressed in town clothes on weekdays. In Hrotovice, a village in the foothills of the Czech-Moravian Highlands, the men wore blue coats to church on Sundays and in the winter they wore yellow furs with tulips embroidered on the back and around the pockets. Women in this village wore short skirts of different colors with red flowers. They wrapped wide blue or black aprons around their skirts, and put on white stockings and white linen scarfs with red or blue flowers for a festive look.[86]

The diet of the rural population reflected the social stratification. Generally, the main components were potatoes and grains cooked in clay pots. Cabbage was another staple, and people ate it raw or pickled in winter months. Dried fruit was popular in most areas. Most families would eat meat only on special occasions (Easter, harvest festivals, and Christmas). The rest of the year the food had a low nutritional value and lacked variety. A cup of weak coffee or soup for breakfast were the daily staples, with a piece of bread and cheese in the evening. On Sunday they had coffee and bread for breakfast, soup and cake for lunch, with a piece of bread for snack. Evening meals were similar to breakfasts.[87] The *sedlák* (wealthy farmer) consumed meat either fresh, following a slaughter of a pig or a cow, or smoked or pickled in salt. Salamies and liver sausages were also made. The most common beverage of all social classes was beer.[88]

The final decision

Despite the strong bonds of family and community that tied Czech peasants to their villages, many lost patience with the constant struggle for a decent livelihood and decided to leave. Some left with regrets and continued to be homesick in the New World. What was the breaking point at which a family or an individual decided to leave? How much or how little, in an abstract sense, did the emigrants from the Czech lands bring with them, and how much of the old culture survived in the brave new world of the American frontier? Did Czechs and Moravians retain their ethnic/national heritages, habits, and characteristics? Or did the great "melting pot" homogenize them into just plain American-style farmers?

In the case of emigrants from Bohemia-Moravia, economic difficulties were probably not a sufficient reason for people to leave their homeland; rather, many factors were at work, including countless social and personal reasons. But once the decision was made and the emigrants left their old homeland to establish themselves in the new world, they took with them many of the customs and attitudes which had shaped their lives in the past and would bring meaning and comfort to the future.

Chapter 3

 The Push to Leave,
the Pull to Stay

To leave or not to leave. That was the question on which the decision of a lifetime hinged for many Czech peasants in the period 1850 to 1900. The previous chapter looked at the general conditions in the Czech lands in the second half of the nineteenth century and focused on the factors that could have precipitated the emigration; this chapter focuses on the individuals who emigrated from the Czech lands and examines the specific influences which impinged upon this crucial decision-making process as these individuals weighed the pros and cons of leaving.

Contemporary studies of decision-making stress the importance of accurate, objective, and comprehensive information—a luxury emigrants in the second half of the nineteenth century did not enjoy. What sources of information did these peasants have at their disposal? How could they counter the dire warnings of Czech nationalists, playwrights, and propagandists who played upon the fear of the unknown which lurks in all of us?

To appreciate the cross-pressures would-be Czech-Moravian emigrants were under, it is also necessary to examine the reactions and opinions of those who chose to stay—peer pressures, presumably, exerted a kind of reverse "pull" that push-pull theorists rarely take into account. The "press" influenced rural Czechs and Moravians to an indeterminate degree. It was clearly present throughout the period under study. But the influence it had on the decision-making processes of those who agonized over whether to go or stay cannot be measured with any precision. Nor was that influence all in one direction. On the contrary, there were countervailing forces at work, and it seems likely that to some extent the conflicting voices of newspapers, pamphlets, letters from friends and relatives in America, and the shipping agents—may have offset one another. The would-be emigrant may have had "help" making his or her decision, but there was plenty of "information" to support either choice, to go or to stay. More fundamental causes, especially the bleak economic prognosis for many poor peasants in the rural areas, were para-mount—with one notable exception. Letters from loved ones ap-pear to have been very instrumental in specific cases in pushing individuals over the edge, so to speak. This phenomenon appears to have been sufficiently common (or even prevalent) as to justify ranking it with socio-economic causes. What this suggests is that for large-scale movement of populations across national boundaries to occur there must be a combination of causes, both long-term (fun-damental, general, or socio-economic) and short-term (immediate, particular, or personal).

Whatever reasons people had for leaving, these facts stand out: a) under the period under examination (1850–1900) Czech emigration surged; b) the emigration virus spread throughout most of rural Bohemia and Moravia (although some areas were hit harder than others); and c) the emigrants represented a broad cross-section of rural Czech-Moravian society with large numbers coming from the cottager class.

Many Czechs left their homeland with a broken heart. Proces-sions of villagers followed them to the railway station. Farewell was sad; many might not have left if they had fully realized the extent of the hardships they would face during the first years on the American frontier. Their personal circumstances varied greatly. Many of them were curious to discover this new country where land was plentiful; many went to escape destitution; some left because their houses burned down; some got married for the second time and wanted to start a life in a new country. Only a few had only one particular reason to leave. Only a few actually knew exactly where they were going; most could hardly imagine the immensity of the American West. Yet thousands of Czechs and Moravians put their belongings into a chest or a blanket and set off on a journey to the German ports and thence across the Atlantic to the New World.

The interplay of unfortunate circumstances

At the railway station in Prague, they were "sitting on their possessions tied up in a bundle," wrote *Katolické listy* (*Catholic Pages*) in 1903, "their faces full of anxiety as they were setting off into the unknown." The article continued, "They would not have said their farewells to their cottages and to their villages if they were not forced to do it by unfortunate circumstances.[1] What were these "unfortunate circumstances"?

"Migration to America is a step upward and onward, consciously and deliberately taken," wrote Kenneth Miller, author of a book on Czechs living in the United States, in 1922.[2] On an individual level, the reasons for migration were often more complex and harder to consciously define than K. Miller suggests, as the testimony of one Czech immigrant who ended up in Milligan, Nebraska, shows: "I had no reason. When I was very small I said that I wanted to come to America."[3] There were at least two kinds of emigrants: those Kenneth Miller wrote about, who acted "consciously and deliberately," and those like the settler in Milligan who claimed to have "no reason."

Both the causes of, and the constraints on, Czech emigration changed over time. The post-1848 emigration was largely political. Activists of 1848 from the Czech lands left for Germany and later for the United States. Political factors later ceased to be the reason for migration, with the exception of a few radical socialist and labor leaders who left for the United States following their expulsion by the Austrian government in the 1880s.[4] The primary causes of emigration in the period 1860–1900, as already noted, were economic.

The demographic survey of 1890

A survey taken by demographers in the Czech lands in 1890 (published in 1912), attempted to identify the reasons for the mass emigration then in progress. The responses came from local government officials and from representatives of banks and insurance companies in the emigration-prone areas.[5]

Demographers found what we have already seen: that the causes of emigration were not only economic, but also social and psychological in the broadest sense. Some people left to escape difficult personal or familial circumstances. Many wanted to escape the military service or a legal action.[6]

The Czech lands had a long history of religious unrest, agitation for reform, and reactionary clerical postures, policies, and attitudes, but religious oppression does not seem to have been a major reason why Czechs and Moravians left their homeland. Even so, the religious nonconformism that was thought to be prevalent in the New World was probably an added attraction for many Bohemian emigrants to the United States. Unlike the Norwegians and some Germans, some Bohemians came to America in search of freedom *from* religion, rather than freedom to practice religious piety.[7]

Apocalypses and epistles

Small-scale catastrophes often prompted villagers to emigrate *en masse*. A chronicle of the village of Lomeč in the Kutná Hora region, located within the high-intensity emigration belt, listed repeated fires occurring in 1866, 1871, and 1880, during which many houses burned down. Cholera, still common in the second half of the nineteenth century, often exacerbated the situation, according to the chronicler of Lomeč.[8]

Information emanating from the New World—a pull factor—played an important role, too. The newspapers published in southern Bohemia and western Moravia advertised the opportunities in the New World. For example, one Czech newspaper carried an advertisement informing readers that the "amount of meat available in Texas, for instance, was more than the quantity of bread available" in Moravia.[9] Between the 1850s and the 1880s, the *Moravské noviny* (*The Moravian News*) occasionally published letters encouraging northern Moravians to emigrate to Texas.

Letters from relatives or neighbors who had emigrated informed peasant-farmers about the prospects of an easy and plentiful life.[10] Europeans were said to be met with warm welcome in the United States.[11] A closer look at two districts in southern Bohemia, the Tábor and Písek districts, showed the strength of the pull the letters exercised.

The emigration from the two districts started early. In 1850, a butcher named A. Lowy left a village near Tábor in southern Bohemia for the United States.[12] (The nostalgia felt by emigrants arriving on the American frontier is memorialized in town names where they settled; the town of Tábor in southeastern South Dakota, for example, was established by people who might have been A. Lowy's neighbors in the old country, or they might simply have wanted to pay homage to the Hussite tradition associated with the original Táborites.)

In 1853, following rumors about a re-introduction of serfdom, emigration began to increase.[13] The first mention of agents' activity in rural Bohemia dates from 1853 and the first publications enticing people to leave were printed in the Bechyně region in the early 1850s.[14]

The Tábor district was soon struck by emigration fever.[15] Between 1855 and 1862, 537 families applied for permission to emigrate. The numbers were probably higher, as much emigration went unrecorded by the administrators.[16]

The requests for permission to leave in most cases mentioned rich relatives or friends living in the United States. Thus a brother was followed by his sibling, his brother-in-law, neighbors from the village, and even relatives from the surrounding villages. Migration developed a snowballing effect in the region of Tábor, at least, but no Czech or Moravian villages were actually transplanted, as happened with some other ethnic groups of emigrants from Europe; furthermore, Táborites, like other Czech emigrants, appear to have dispersed upon arrival on America's shores.

Letters informed the would-be emigrants about the needs of the American job market. "As artisans such as a blacksmith, carpenter, and bricklayer are needed in the United States, I believe that I should do well for myself and for my family," F. Dvořák, a blacksmith from Radĕnín wrote in his request for emigration in 1855.[17]

Matĕj Pejrša, a cottager and a laborer from the Tábor district, left with his wife and four children in 1860. His brother Jan, who followed Matĕj seven years later, wrote in his application for the permission to leave that Matĕj was able to buy a piece of land, build a house, and homestead. Matĕj encouraged Jan to come to the United States where he would support him and give him a piece of land.[18]

Many applicants for permission to leave could not have emigrated to the United States without the help of their relatives. Many were young laborers or hired hands (*čeledín*). In 1879, Jan Matuška, a twenty-four-year-old unmarried laborer, received a letter from his "good friends living a comfortable life in Chicago who wish to look

after me when I get there." Matuška soon left for America.[19] Josef
Hogan, a thirty-year-old *čeledín*, left with his three children and wife.
His friends already living in the United States paid for the journey.[20]
Laborer Josef Kotrba, single, decided to leave for the United States
in 1878. "My friends in the United States have been able to live well
through hard work," he wrote in his application, "and they promised
to help me also." He expressed fears about remaining in his homeland common to many applications:

> I would not be able to support myself and I am afraid that in
> the next few years I shall not be able to live off my good
> friends because economic conditions are so bad. I have
> given up trying to improve the situation. In the United
> States I shall work hard and be frugal and there I shall be able
> to make a good living and save money.[21]

František Tříska, thirty-eight years old, worried that while
now he had enough to eat, "in the near future the situation might
change. Opportunities for employment are disappearing." Giving
up any hope for a better life in Bohemia, Tříska left for the United
States and settled in Nebraska.[22]

Czech-American settlers often sent money or a ticket to their
relatives, or promised to help new immigrants secure employment
in the United States.[23] Sometimes a wealthy Czech settler who had
had several members of a family working for him in Bohemia would
pay the passage for the whole family as a way to get cheap labor in
America.[24] Anna Cunát became a beggar after her husband, František,
son of a poor laborer, emigrated. In her application, she stated that
she had tickets purchased by unnamed "relatives" in America.[25]

Peasants, maids, a variety of workmen, craftsmen, and artisans
appear frequently among the applicants to emigrate. The majority
of applicants, however, were laborers (*čeledín*)—the result of a
population explosion, and of the post-1848 situation in Czech
villages when abolishing of servitude freed many peasants. This
trend remained unchanged for the next several decades. The surplus of laborers in some regions was extremely high. In 1858, to cite
an example, the administration of one village requested the Tábor
district administration not to give marriage licenses to *čeledín* since
children in families with small incomes could not support themselves and were a burden to the village community. In many
instances leaders of a village supported requests to emigrate to be rid
of the unwanted poor.

Letters appear to have ignited a kind of migrational chain-reaction in some villages, but memoirs and letters written by Czech-American settlers show that people who had been living in the same village or close to one another sometimes met each other quite by accident in the United States, and expressed great surprise at such chance meetings.[26]

Many letters in circulation in villages were false, often planted by agents working for steamship companies. Most agents operated from the German ports under unofficial protection of the local governments in Bremen and Hamburg who realized the economic benefits emigration brought to the ports.[27] They travelled "under cover" throughout the country, pretending to be teachers, innkeepers, and office clerks, and disseminating propaganda on the good life that awaited Czech emigrants to America.[28]

The Ministry of Foreign Affairs for the Austro-Hungarian Empire kept records of the agents' misconduct. For example, one document showed that an alleged agent deceived customers by taking money for services he did not provide.[29] Archival material in Vienna shows that the energy the Austrian government devoted to the monitoring agents was considerable.[30]

Although agents were a factor in encouraging emigration, an investigation of several sending districts in Bohemia, further supported by archival documents in Vienna, Hamburg, and Bremen, revealed that in "only a small fraction of cases (ten percent at the most) was an emigration mediated by agents residing in the country."[31] In reality, the agents were made scapegoats by the real culprits—the bureaucrats—who failed to address the social and economic problems that were the root causes of emigration from rural Bohemia and Moravia.

Emigration was legal from 1867 on, but the government wanted to control it and stop steamship agents from recruiting young men liable for military service to go overseas.[32] District military commands, however, were benevolent towards the emigration of reservists, who normally received permission to emigrate.[33] In 1880 sometimes twenty-year-old men could emigrate if they had serious reasons.[34]

The exodus gains momentum: who migrated and why

Besides the groups of rural emigrants discussed earlier—the middling farmers, owners of the ever-shrinking plots of land, and those of the young generation unwilling to face the hardships that their parents had to endure—there were many farm laborers who left because they saw no chance of improving their lot in life if they stayed. Landless peasants in Bohemia, they hoped to become self-reliant farmers in America. The operative word is "hope"—in America they saw hope. The prospect of working as *čeledín* all their lives, as latter-day serfs, was especially unappealing to the youth of rural Bohemia-Moravia.[35]

Most emigrants were young married men with children. The average age of the fifty-four emigrants from the Milevsko region of south Bohemia was 30.7 years. Most of them were laborers. The rest represented a virtual cross-section of the typical village workforce: blacksmiths, mill-hands, tailors' assistants, weavers. Most (68.5 percent) were encouraged to emigrate by their relatives or friends already in the United States, and it would seem probable that among the poor segments of the rural society the pull of relatives living in the United States was decisive.

The chronicle of Lomeč, a small village of about four hundred people within the emigration-prone area, explicitly stated that the local youth did not want to countenance the hard-scrabble existence that lay in store for them and therefore many decided to leave.[36]

Even skilled laborers feared that they would not be able to find jobs at home. Many hoped that they would be paid more for their skills in the United States.[37]

People past their productive age were also leaving, usually with the young ones to help them on the farm. Retired parents living on their children's property (*vyměnkáři*) had given up the ownership of the house or farm to their children, who were responsible for supporting them in their old age. These older peasants, locked in their socio-economic group, could no longer become wealthy because everything they had owned had been passed on to their children. Thus, for some older Czechs, going to America was probably a quest for lost youth and a last chance to reclaim their dignity and independence.

The empire strikes back: Vienna's response

From Vienna's perspective, the Czech emigration threatened to become a mass exodus in the 1870s. The government had to do something. But what?

Emigration was small in the first half of the nineteenth century, but as the trickle became a steady stream the government tried to counter this trend through a policy of internal colonization: to settle depopulated areas within the empire. The reason for Vienna's concern was partly psychological and partly military. Psychologically, the fact that people were choosing to leave suggested that there was something wrong with the empire, perhaps even that it was in decay—not a pleasant thought for the imperial government in Vienna. Militarily, the size of a state's population was still directly linked with its war-making capacity in the second half of the nineteenth century.

Land armies had always been crucial in determining the outcome of conflict on the continent. In 1866, for instance, the Prussians had defeated Austria in a war in which the major battle had been fought near Konnigratz (Hradec Králove), located in eastern Bohemia. Hence, demographics were a matter of vital concern to Emperor Franz Josef (1848–1916), who was faced with two major challenges: liberalism and the emergent German state (the Second Reich). And, of course, Vienna was acutely aware of the fact that young men of military service age were the ones most likely to leave.

Imperial anxieties over the population question were reflected in law and policy from the early 1840s. Vienna first decreed an internal colonization law in 1843, during an unemployment crisis, and another one in 1846. In the 1850s, the imperial government promulgated a law to colonize the less developed and sparsely populated Hungarian part of the empire. The intention failed, as the only positive response came from the rural poor south of Prague.[38] The non-Slavic Hungarians (Magyars) probably did not welcome the possibility of a Czech and Moravian intrusion into their territory.

Prior to 1848, freedom to emigrate was limited and the process of obtaining permission to leave complicated, but not impossible. The government considered illegal emigrants to be criminals and, according to the law of August 10, 1784, could legally confiscate their property. (At that time, peasants were still serfs and therefore treated as property; they had no rights whatever.) By restricting population movement, the emperor wanted to stop migration of skilled artisans vital for the development of manufacturing. He also did not want them to take their skills abroad (an early version of the "brain drain" that has been a major concern in the Third World and elsewhere in the second half of the twentieth century). This restrictive legislation was renewed in 1832, a reaction to the increase in illegal emigration in the first decades of the nineteenth century.

In 1867, Franz Joseph decided to remove barriers to emigration, a change that was part of the liberalization in the empire following Austria's defeat at the hands of Prussia in 1866.[39] The change in the law on emigration was not so much a sign of the government's benevolence as a recognition of existing realities and an attempt to accommodate to adversity. By the late 1860s emigration became a mass phenomenon that could not be stopped. The law of 1867 decreed a general amnesty for the naturalized American citizens who had emigrated to escape military service.[40] The Austrian government, however, continued to check male emigrants-to-be to see if they had served a military term.[41]

The demographers whose task was to survey the high-emigration areas proposed a number of progressive measures designed to stop the population hemorrhage. Besides suggesting the need to improve the general standard of living, they thought that the poor agricultural areas should be industrialized. Small-holding peasants should be helped with the payment of their debts and greater equity in land ownership should be achieved by breaking up large estates. The aristocracy, which owned most of the land, should be abolished, and the peasants should share the available land. Cooperatives should support artisans and their crafts. Weakening the clerics' grip on peasants' lives would also shake them out of their tradition-bound lethargy and set the stage for greater self-reliance and individualism. "When we have America here, the people will stop moving there," concluded the demographers.[42]

The question "When will it stop?" probably accounts for the alarm over the emigration issue. The following table shows the trend of Czech emigration to the United States in the second half of the nineteenth century. The peak came (as noted earlier) during the decade 1870–1880:

Increase in Bohemian-born population in the United States, 1860–1900.			
1860–1870	1870–1880	1880–1890	1890–1900
33,000	50,000	62,000	42,000
—	(45,072)	(32,745)	(38,785)

Source: U.S. Congress, Senate, U.S. Immigration Commission, 61st Cong., 3d sess., 1911, Vol. 3, 417.

Note: Figures compiled by V. Mastny (1962), and Professor Josef Polišenský of Charles University in Prague, from the United States Census records, Austrian governmental records, and data from the emigration offices in Bremen and Hamburg. In parentheses are the figures from U.S. Immigration Commission [Dillingham Commission, 1911].

Although the absolute numbers of Czechs and Moravians who left in any given decade were relatively modest, emigration was a problem for a small nation which for centuries had struggled for an independent development from neighboring nations. For instance, the conservative *Katolické Listy* (*Catholic Pages*) blamed the Austrian government for the dire economic climate that was ultimately causing the emigration. The author of the article called for long overdue national, political, and economic reforms that would limit the emigration.[43] This growing disenchantment with Vienna over the latter's seeming inability to stop the hemorrhaging that was weakening Bohemia coincided with the emergence of a national reawakening in the Czech lands.

The Czech National Revival Movement

Czech leaders did not have the legal authority or political power to stem the outflow, but it is clear from various sources that they opposed emigration on nationalistic grounds.[44] These leaders came from the upper class and were instrumental in the *národní obrození* ("national revival") movement of the eighteenth and early nineteenth centuries. They were struggling to keep the Czech culture and language alive and to set it on an equal footing with the

German culture that had long dominated in the Czech lands. The growing power of the Second Reich no doubt intensified the fear of impending Germanization. Most important administrative offices and businesses were in the hands of officials or individuals whose native language was German, not Czech. And most landowners were foreign aristocrats.

Czech intellectuals saw in the Czech peasantry "the core of the nation," the backbone of the Czech culture, and the keeper of the Czech identity and language. Czech and Moravian villages had indeed kept alive the national folklore through the "long winter" of German and Habsburg domination.

For the Czech liberal bourgeoisie, the reasons behind the Czech rural emigration were quite incomprehensible. For these patriots, Czech nationalism was an inspiring ideal, one closely linked to the liberal reforms (including constitutionalism, civil rights, and national self-determination) which they so ardently sought. Czech liberals attributed the high rate of emigration to weakened patriotic feelings on the part of the peasantry.[45] They failed to understand that peasants needed to eat in order to think about an abstraction like the nation and patriotism.

But idealism and national fervor were not the only considerations. The aspiring Czech bourgeoisie had many of the same interests as entrepreneurs elsewhere. By the late 1880s, when many emigrants were unskilled laborers, they wanted to insure an abundant supply of cheap labor to keep wages down.

Opposition to emigration came from other sectors of society as well. For example, women who were members of *Ústřední výbor českých žen* (Central Committee of the Czech Women) warned against the decline of the population caused by the emigration. They thought that the emigrants were mainly male and thus they expressed a concern over an uneven distribution of sexes. They were afraid that while young people were more likely to leave, the unproductive stratum of the population was growing. While these concerns were not entirely fatuous, the statistics suggest that Czech-Moravian emigration was fairly well balanced between the sexes, with only slightly more males than females leaving. By no means was there the kind of gross imbalance some Czech critics claimed.

One writer and prominent figure in the Czech national revival movement, Josef Kajetán Tyl, imagined the ordeal the Czechs had to undergo in the wide open spaces in the upper Mississippi valley. Tyl wrote a theatrical satire *Lesní panna aneb cesta do Ameriky* (*A Sprite, or, A Journey to America*). The play warned against deceitful agents who lied to attract people to the New World, and depicted the misconceptions and the reality of an American experience:[46]

> Americans have dances all the time because every-
> thing they desire falls from the sky. Many are impa-
> tient here because life is so hard; they want to go to
> America where dumplings grow on trees. Underneath
> those trees are lakes filled with butter and the dump-
> lings can be dipped in that butter if you cannot eat
> them easily. Pigs are roasted and pigeons and birds are
> already fried when they fly, cakes and koláče bake by
> themselves and coffee pours straight into the mouth .
> .. America is painted in such beautiful colors, what a
> shame that it is so far and so expensive to get there! .
> .. Americans cannot be lazy because they need to work
> to be alive as we need to, those who do not want to
> work cannot eat . . . [47]

The same publisher printed Czech versions of German short stories with similar themes. Works entitled "Emigrants to America" and "Emigrants to Brazil," among others, show how the anti-emigration forces used short stories to discourage people from leaving.[48]

At the height of the emigration in the 1880s, the press, with only a few exceptions, joined the Czech nationalists in condemning emigration. "Všude chleba o dvou kůrkach" (bread has only two crusts no matter where one goes) was a commonly used proverb. The authors of articles stressed that hard work was a necessity in America as elsewhere, that there was no "easy street" awaiting those who dared to leave. [49]

General opinion in the Czech lands was that the government must take action to improve the economic situation and remove the root causes of emigration. The press criticized the Austrian govern-ment for not subsidizing schools that would teach the modern techniques of agricultural production, and called on the government to invest in irrigation, the regulation of rivers, and the development of an efficient railroad network. Articles in newspapers also called for a modernization of the credit system for peasants.[50]

In 1880, the editor of a liberal national paper read mainly by the middle class, *Národní listy* (*National Pages*), saw the main cause of emigration in the surplus of unemployed work force generated by mechanization of industries that put out of work thousands of weavers.[51] A similar attitude could be heard on the other side of the ocean in Nebraska's *Pokrok Západu* (*Progress of the West*) in 1880: the population in the Czech lands had been growing at such a pace that the surplus labor force had to leave. The author visualized the country as a beehive that was constantly being left by young bees who were flying somewhere else, in search of new settlements in the United States in which the Czech people were likely to drown in the English element.[52]

Writing in the same year, the author of an article in *České noviny* (*Czech News*) conceded that the peasants might eventually do well in the United States, but warned that it took an average of ten years to own a piece of land there.[53] Three years later, in 1883, a writer in the same newspaper cautioned prospective emigrants against migrating by stressing the need to work twice as hard in the United States because the competition within the work force was high there, and by stressing that giving up Czech customs and traditions and knowing the English language was imperative if one were to become an American. The author was evidently reacting to the nativist sentiment and xenophobia in certain areas of the United States.[54] The nativist sentiment and the trend to restrict the European immigration was an added fuel to writers of anti-emigration articles. In 1887 a writer in *Česká politika* (*Czech Politics*) pointed to American workers' organizations designed to fight the influx of emigrants and the U.S. government's policy banning poor and undesirable immigrants.[55]

At the height of the rural emigration at the end of the 1880s, some newspapers with predominantly agrarian readerships reacted to the flight of the rural population. In an 1889 article entitled "Should we emigrate to the United States?" *Rolnické listy* (*Peasant Newspaper*), published in an area with a high rate of emigration, described the difficulties connected with emigration. A peasant had to sell his property and deal with agents before the journey. Then came the sea-sickness during the journey itself. The author went on to say that not everybody was suited for America, where people often had to work hard at jobs that might be embarrassing or humiliating to these same people in Bohemia. The best public lands in the United States had been taken, and the only land left was in desolate regions. Therefore if a peasant were industrious, saved money, and did not drink excessively, he/she would be better off staying at home.[56]

The issue of preserving Czech culture was never far beneath the surface in this outpouring of anti-emigration literature. For example, the "permanent loss to the Czech nation," was addressed by an editor writing for *Národní listy* (*National Pages*) in 1884. He lamented that Czechs had no voice in American politics, and that the Czech language would be forgotten since Czech was taught only in elementary schools and only in a few areas, and was spoken only during the church services.[57]

The anti-emigration propaganda also reached the shores of the United States via Czech newspapers. In 1881 Josef Pačas from Schuyler, Nebraska, in a commentary for *Pokrok Západu* reacted to an anti-emigration article in *Brněnské noviny* (*Brno News*). Although money was not lying in the streets in America, Pačas wrote, hard-working people would do well.[58] In Europe, unlike in the United States, fate played an important role in the thinking of people, Pačas continued. Wealth and status were predetermined by some unshakable force, and an alteration of an individual's social status was impossible. Pačas thought his years spent in the native country had been wasted. He could not provide for his family on the money he earned, the taxes were too high, and borrowing was ruinous. Pačas reported that work in the United States was easier than in Bohemia. People were independent-minded individuals in America and no-body had to listen to the commands of a land baron who determined even the times when the workers could eat. The wealthy farmer in Bohemia would enjoy roast meat with his family while the farm hands had to do with a piece of bread, and they would still be required to work in the afternoon, according to the author, disillu-sioned about life in the old country.[59]

While Pačas was a success story, many might not have left if they had fully realized the extent of the hardships they would face during the first years on the American frontier. Only a few knew exactly where they were going. Most could hardly imagine the immensity of the American West.

Part II

Into the
New World

Chapter 4

 Endless Horizons:
Settlement and Occupa-
tional Patterns of Early
Czechs in America

Czechs did not immigrate to America in large numbers until the 1870s. In 1850 a mere five hundred Czech immigrants had arrived on the shores of the New World.[1] By 1900 the number had swelled to 200,000.[2] Thus, the ancestors of the vast majority of Czech-Americans today came to this country during the second half of the nineteenth century. It is no accident that this was precisely the time when the Great American West—the frontier—was opening. It is also the time when the Age of Imperialism reached its zenith. For the great powers of Europe, territorial expansion could only come in one of two ways: by war and conquest on the continent or by colonization of lands and peoples in faraway places.[3] But for the United States of America, the empire that beckoned was always just beyond the horizon. And there were always natural boundaries that seemed almost ordained by the Almighty: first the Mississippi River, then the Rocky Mountains, and finally, the Pacific Ocean. The endless horizon of the American frontier attracted thousands upon thousands of Czech immigrants in the last three decades of the nineteenth century.

Although the scale of this population movement was unprecedented, migration was not a new phenomenon for Bohemians and

Moravians. Pre-1850 emigration had had a political character. Many Czech political leaders had fled to escape Austrian oppression. Following the defeat of Czech Protestants by the Austrian Habsburgs (the Austrian ruling dynasty) at the Battle of White Mountain in 1620, several prominent leaders of the revolt joined Swedish and Dutch trading companies and sailed for America in the 1630s. In 1740 Moravian Brethren—a mixture of Czechs and Germans—left the Czech lands to escape religious persecution in the aftermath of the Thirty Years' War and settled in small numbers in Pennsylvania, Georgia, and Virginia. Later, after the Revolution of 1848, political persecution prompted several hundred Czech radicals to emigrate.[4] The stream of Czech immigration was slowed by the worldwide economic crisis of 1857 and then stopped completely for the duration of the American Civil War.[5]

Immigration, the Homestead Act, and divine intervention

The second and third waves of immigration came in the early 1870s and 1880s. If it is true that coincidences are really God's way of remaining anonymous, then perhaps the great Czech immigrations in the 1870s and 1880s were the result of divine intervention. In any event, it so happened that the Homestead Act of 1862, by opening the vast unsettled expanses of territory on the American Great Plains just when the pressures for emigration in Czech lands reached their peak, set the stage for the Czechs' mass exodus from Bohemia and Moravia in the decades that followed the American Civil War. Of course, the Homestead Act greatly influenced settlement patterns on the frontier as well. Czech immigrants, like many others, were attracted primarily by the prospect of abundant and affordable land, a prospect that had long ago faded in the Old Country.

The third Czech immigration wave peaked in 1891 when the number of Czech immigrants to the United States exceeded 11,000.[6] Czech immigration continued until 1914, but pales in comparison with the hundreds of thousands who immigrated from the other provinces of the Habsburg monarchy and from southern and eastern Europe.[7]

The figures in the following table are composites based on the United States Census records, Austrian governmental records, and data from the emigration offices of Bremen and Hamburg. The numbers are approximate since the record taking was different in the three countries. Offices in the United States, for instance, recorded the place of origin while Austria used the country of last permanent residence. The numbers indicate, however, the trends.

Immigration from the Czech lands, 1850–1900:		
	Number of Czech immigrants	% of all emigration from the Austrian Empire
1850–60	23,000	63%
1861–70	33,000	83%
1871–80	50,000	57%
1881–90	62,000	25%
1890–1900	42,000	10%

Source: Josef Polišenský, "*Obecné problémy dějin českého vystěhovalectví, 1850–1914,*" (*General problems of the Czech migration history*) 1987 TMs [photocopy], 16, received from the author. (Based on Vojtěch Mastný's data.)

In general, the data show that Czech immigration grew in absolute numbers until the last decade of the nineteenth century, although it decreased as a proportion of total immigration from the Habsburg Empire. After 1880, Czech immigrants were part of a larger influx from the empire; prior to 1880 they were leading the way.[8]

All roads to America pass through Germany

An overwhelming majority of Czechs and Moravians came directly from the Austro-Hungarian Empire. A small number of Czechs had resided elsewhere—mainly in Germany—before they decided to emigrate to the United States.[9]

A ticket from Prague to Omaha via Chicago cost fifty-six dollars in 1881. The German ports of Bremen and Hamburg were the main train terminals and embarkation points for Czechs and Moravians making the voyage to America. The Kareš and Stocký firm representing North-German Lloyd in Bremen, with agents in

Bohemia, outdistanced the British company operating from Liverpool in attracting passengers from the Czech lands.[10]

Most ships leaving from Germany went to New York, Baltimore, and Boston. New Orleans and Galveston served as ports of entry for Czechs intending to settle in St. Louis or Texas. Some Czechs arrived in New Orleans and went via the Mississippi and Missouri Rivers to Omaha.

Ports and cities where immigrants landed had agents to help them. Few agencies had a genuinely altruistic mission. One notable exception was the Czech-Slav Immigrant House set up by a local Czech organization in Baltimore during the peak of the Czech immigration in the 1870s and 1880s. The center gave immigrants free advice, provided accommodations, and helped them to connect with kinfolk and friends.[11]

The American dream: city slicker or country squire?

The oldest Czech settlements were in New York, St. Louis, and Cleveland. For a majority of the immigrants, New York was only a gateway to the New World, because the cost of living in New York and in the cities along the Atlantic was considerably higher than in the area of the Great Lakes and the Midwest.[12] In 1870, 1,487 Czechs lived in New York City. Many worked in the small-scale production of luxury items. Three-fourths of the first-generation Czechs worked in the tobacco industry, but that number declined in the second generation.[13]

The influx of Czech mass migration in the early 1850s came out of western and south-western Bohemia and settled mainly in Cleveland, St. Louis, and Chicago. Czechs "discovered" Cleveland and St. Louis at about the same time. St. Louis had the highest concentration of Czechs prior to the American Civil War. During the war all the southern transport routes were cut off, and Chicago became more attractive, particularly when rail transportation made it a major east-west link in the 1860s.

According to the directory listings, Cleveland had three Czech families in 1850, fifteen in 1860, and 696 in 1869, which amounted to 3,252 persons.[14] Information about these early immigrants is sketchy. While St. Louis attracted Catholics, Cleveland had a large freethinking population. Most of these Czechs came from the villages near towns of Písek, Tábor, and České Budějovice in southern Bohemia.[15]

The settlement and behavioral patterns of the Cleveland Czechs were typical of Czech enclaves in other cities. Czechs formed little islands in which the immigrants perpetuated their social and cultural traditions and heritage. The names of the Czech districts in Cleveland, such as "Little Bohemia," Prague, and Plzeň, indicated the strength of the ties to their homeland. In a pattern that would be replicated later elsewhere in the Midwest, Czechs in Cleveland tended to settle near Germans.[16] The fact that German was the official language of the Austro-Hungarian Empire and many Czechs, no doubt, had some familiarity with German words and ways, may account, in part, for this tendency.

The Czech population in Chicago grew even more rapidly than that in Cleveland. The production of agricultural machines started in Chicago in 1841; the railroad and the meat packing houses provided employment opportunities for immigrant workers starting in the 1860s.[17] In 1863 there were seven thousand Czechs; two years later the number had grown to ten thousand.[18] By the time the Dillingham Commission made its survey of immigrants in 1911, 40 percent of Czechs and Moravians had lived there for over twenty years. Chicago continued to be an attractive city for immigrants even after the turn of the century; 20 percent of the Czechs had been residing there for less than five years. In time, Czechs became the fifth most numerous ethnic group living in the city.[19]

The first Czechs came to Chicago in 1852. Most came from the old emigration areas of southwestern and southern Bohemia, from the villages near Písek, Vodňany, and Tábor. A few came from an area east of Prague. A later wave of Czech immigrants came predominantly from small urban areas such as Turnov, northern Bohemia, and Vysoké Mýto and Pardubice in eastern Bohemia.[20]

Many Czechs only stayed in Chicago temporarily before moving on to the West. Some did not like the urban atmosphere and many were drawn westward by the allure of free land and the frontier. Czechs with professional skills had difficulties in learning the English language, a factor that excluded many from a labor pool in urban settings, particularly if they sought white-collar employment. Only a few found employment in Czech businesses.

In chronology and destinations Czech immigration resembles that of Scandinavians and Germans. For all three, farming was the most attractive occupation. The rural character of Czech immigration distinguishes the Czechs from other Slavs,[21] who settled in large numbers in cities because they favored urban life or arrived too late to take advantage of the Homestead Act lands which were staked in the main by Scandinavians, Germans, and Czechs, and, of course, Americans who took Horace Greeley's advice to "go West young man, go West."[22]

Survival skills: making it in America

Czechs were a small portion of the total immigrants. First-generation Czechs as a proportion of the male labor force amounted to a mere 0.3 percent. Nonetheless, Czechs were successful in several occupational pursuits; as tailors, tobacco and cigar factory operatives, and as leather-case makers, all jobs requiring skills.[23] Cottagers constituted the majority of Czech immigrants, and one characteristic of this class was that they possessed useful skills. Bringing these skills to America helped the newcomers survive economically.

The trend among Czechs in terms of occupational pursuits saw a growing number working in agriculture, and a declining number in manufacturing by 1900 (32 percent of first-generation Bohemians in the United States were employed in agricultural pursuits; and 42 percent in the second generation). Surprisingly, the number of self-employed farmers actually declined while the number of paid laborers in agriculture rose in the second generation. The explanation is most likely that young second-generation males sought employment as hired hands hoping eventually to get some land of their own. The Swedes experienced the same trend, but the proportion of Germans in agriculture, as noted above, remained about the same (27 percent and 28 percent). In 1920, 77 percent of Czechs were employed in farming, which was 3.2 percent of the whole population of immigrant farmers. The numbers are proportionately higher for Czechs than for the English, Scotch, Welsh, and Germans.[24]

Not surprisingly, the highest proportion of first-generation Czech immigrants worked in manufacturing—fully 40 percent. (For the second generation, this number is 10 percent lower.) Another significant concentration was in personal and domestic services. Sixteen percent of the first generation worked in this field; 10 percent of the second generation.[25] As noted earlier, many first-generation Czechs were employed in the tobacco industry; these people were no doubt "transplants," i.e., they came from a locale in Bohemia where tobacco processing was done and sought similar employment in America.[26]

Almost half of Czech females of both generations were in manufacturing and mechanical pursuits. One-third of Czech women were in domestic services, a trend that persisted into the second generation.[27] By comparison, over half of first-generation German women worked in domestic services, but in the second generation this rate was considerably lower (35 percent). One-quarter of German women of the first generation were employed in manufacturing, and the number rose to almost 40 percent in the second generation.[28]

The Czechs who wanted to work in agriculture found the eastern part of America a formidable challenge. The soil was already exhausted and had to be fertilized before it would produce. Farmers had to specialize in a commercial crop to survive, and many simply lacked the knowledge and skills to specialize. Some settlements were too far from the railroads, which made transportation of produce difficult and expensive. These conditions sounded too much like the hard-scrabble existence they had left behind; therefore not many Czech farmers decided to stay in the East.[29]

Prior to coming to the United States, 36 percent of the Czech population in Chicago had been engaged in farming. Relative to other ethnic groups this number was not very high; only Swedes, Jews, and Germans had a lower percentage. Only 17 percent of Swedes had been engaged in farming prior to coming to the United States. Slovaks had a clearly rural background since 85 percent farmed in the Old Country.[30]

The income of Czechs and Moravians varied with location; in Chicago, for example, it was considerably lower than most other ethnic groups. The average income of Czech male heads of households was $472, second lowest to Italians. Swedes earned $516, Poles $517, and Irish $573. The income earnings of Germans was $603.[31] In Cleveland, however, the income of Czechs, though a little lower, was in relative terms among the highest ($450). The native-born earned about $300 more.[32]

The lure of the West

Letters from the United States to relatives and friends had stimulated Czech immigration to the midwestern states. Colonization clubs centered in Chicago, where shipping companies and railroad agents facilitated them.[33] Once Czechs settled in an area, the future Czech-American generations could be found in the same area or nearby, for Czech youth rarely moved far from where they were raised. If they did move to another area it was usually due to a colonizing effort initiated by "older" Czech settlers. Through it all, the degree of "ethnic cohesion" remained high.[34]

By the turn of the nineteenth century a third of the total of approximately 350,000 first- and second-generation Czech immigrants in the United States worked in agriculture in the Midwest— Wisconsin, Minnesota, Iowa, South and North Dakota—and in Texas.[35]

The oldest rural settlements were in Texas and Wisconsin. Following its annexation in 1845, Texas became a magnet for migration. Czech Protestants (Czech Brethren) were the first group to settle in Burleson County, Texas, prior to 1848. Immigrants fleeing after the 1848 Revolution came in the early 1850s to Fayette County, Texas, via Galveston. By 1900, Texas had approximately 3,000 second-generation Czech and Moravian farmers and 538 first-generation (about 15 percent of all farmers from the Czech lands in the United States), settled in about thirty Czech settlements in twelve counties.[36]

The oldest Czech settlement in Wisconsin originated in 1844 in Caledonia. Four years later, Racine, Wisconsin, was almost synonymous with Czechs. These newcomers were young and came from wealthy classes. They were spurred by their political convictions and came in the aftermath of the 1848 Revolution.[37] Most of the early immigrants came from an area around Tábor and Plzeň.[38] Domažlice in southwestern Bohemia was the source of immigration to Manitowoc and to Brown County. These immigrants were wealthy Czechs who came to farm. By 1900 there were 2,751 first-generation farmers (20 percent of the whole Czech population in the state) in Wisconsin and 865 (1 percent) second-generation.[39]

The best land in Wisconsin could be purchased for $1.25 an acre in the frontier years.[40] As a result, early settlers to Wisconsin often became wealthy because they had bought land at affordable prices and, through land speculation, gained a windfall.

Tomáš Čapek found that in the 1860s Wisconsin was widely advertised by Austrian and German newspapers for settlement.[41] The state was free of slave labor—an unwelcome competition for Czechs. Also, the climate was favorable for growing familiar crops. But the Homestead Act of 1862 opened little free land in Wisconsin because the best land had already been bought. By 1870 Wisconsin was well-populated, and the immigrants coming later found most of the desirable land taken. The timing was unfortunate for these latecomers. They often came from the lower economic strata in the Old Country and had little or no money; as land values rose, they were priced out of the market.

Land was still available in the 1870s in Kewaunee County, north of Manitowoc, where many Czechs decided to settle.[42] Josef Svoboda, one such settler, had followed a complicated route from a small Bohemian village to Kewaunee. Born in the foothills of the Czech-Moravian Highlands southeast of Prague, the son of a poor weaver who could not afford to pay for his son's education, Svoboda decided to go to Vienna. There Svoboda worked with his uncle as a cabinet-maker's apprentice. His profession took him to the Balkans, and a sense of adventure prompted him to leave for the United States in 1881. He went first to Chicago and eventually made his way to Kewaunee County, no doubt attracted by the prospect of acquiring a piece of land he could call his own.[43]

Some Czech settlers came to Wisconsin from Texas following the Civil War.[44] But they discovered to their dismay that they were too late—the price of land was too expensive. Many Czechs from Wisconsin joined the westward movement in search of cheap land; most of these Czechs settled in Iowa, Kansas, and Nebraska.[45] By 1900, some 14,145 Bohemians had permanently settled in Wisconsin; the largest concentrations of Czechs were in Milwaukee, Kewaunee, and Manitowoc.[46]

The state of Wisconsin was in the forefront of Czech political, social, and cultural activity in the second half of the nineteenth century. The most famous Czech immigrant, Vojtěch Náprstek, although not a permanent settler, came to Milwaukee in 1848 as a political emigre. Upon his return to Prague in 1857, having made many valuable contacts in America, he established a center for the study of Czechs living abroad that housed a museum of the Americas and a library. There he started a collection of all the materials produced by Czech emigrants, and "devoted the rest of his life to familiarizing his countrymen with America."[47] This center, which is still operating today in Old Town in the center of Prague, remains a vital resource for scholars interested in studying the history of Czech emigration.

Czechs came to Minnesota in the late 1850s from the towns of Tábor, Bechyně, and Veselí in southern Bohemia. Many immigrants from the Czech lands were attracted by the areas covered with timber because, according to Milan Woodrow Jerabek, "the ownership of forest land was to them a symbol of lordship and power, for in Bohemia practically all the forests were owned by the nobility."[48]

The biggest wave arrived in the 1860s. They came either directly from Bohemia-Moravia, or via Illinois or Wisconsin in a migration that progressed in stages. For example, Josef Vondra arrived in Manchester, Iowa, in 1860. He bought a piece of land which he did not like. In 1867 he and a group of other disenchanted Czechs left the area for Minnesota.[49] They used oxen and covered wagons. They were happier on the wooded land around New Prague where they decided to stay, probably because the town had many Czech settlers.[50]

Czechs settled near Hopkins in rural Hennepin County, and in the Minnesota River valley.[51] Although these early Czech immigrants came mainly from the rural districts of eastern and southern Bohemia, the adjustment to the enchanting landscape with lakes and large wooded areas of Minnesota was difficult. The winters were severe. The land had to be cleared before the plough could be used. Markets were not easily accessible, as the railroad was not built until during the Civil War.[52] To support their families during the first difficult years, many men left for months at a time to work in the cities—a strategy followed by many Czechs in later years in the rest of the Midwest.[53]

Generally, the early Czech immigrants were concentrated in the southeast section of Minnesota. By the turn of the century Czechs settled in the southwest part of the state where there was still land available. At that time Minnesota had 11,147 Czech settlers, of whom 2,462 were first-generation farmers (22 percent) and 640 were second-generation (6 percent).[54] Ramsey, Le Seuer, and McLeod Counties had the largest concentration of Czechs.[55]

The first Czechs arrived in eastern Iowa in 1850. The number of Czechs grew rapidly: at the turn of the century there were around forty thousand Czechs settled in Iowa, over three thousand were farmers of the first two generations.[56] Most of these settlers came from eastern Bohemia and western Moravia. Further Czech settlement of Iowa and the rest of the midwestern states was stimulated by settlers' letters to their relatives and friends, and facilitated by colonization clubs centered in Chicago, by shipping companies, and by railroad agents.[57] The Iowa State Immigration Agency, for instance, had an office in New York with sub-agents working in Europe.[58]

In the early 1860s, a group from Pardubice area, eastern Bohemia, settled in Linn County. The group made the ocean crossing with about four hundred Germans and with six families from Kutná Hora.[59] They landed in New York and set off on a six-day train journey to Iowa. After a stop in Chicago, they were welcomed to Iowa by several families whom they had known from Bohemia. Josef Kostlán was a member of the group. Kostlán described how he met people whom he had known at home and how he re-discovered neighbors from villages near his birthplace. They had not made plans to go to America together, but it seems that the situation was unbearable for many and so they independently made the same decision to leave for the United States.

In Iowa as in other midwestern states, Czechs settled near Germans. Although in Europe there were mutual animosities between the two nationalities in the realm of the Habsburg Monarchy, the political situation in North America was different from that in Europe, and Czechs probably felt close to an ethnic group that they had known from Europe and whose language many Czechs could understand.

Whether the German penchant for land acquisition might have influenced the Czechs—whether, in other words, the Czechs were imitating the Germans—is an intriguing question for which, unfortunately, there is no answer. In any event, Germans appear to have eased the adjustment for Czechs, acting as a kind of buffer between an alien host society and a group of Bohemian expatriates who, in many cases, could speak but little English and had no knowledge of American frontier folkways.

While they were establishing themselves, Czechs worked for German farmers, who had been settled in Iowa longer than Czechs. The customs were similar but Czechs allegedly "lacked the cool-natured endurance of the northern Germans."[60] Women earned their living as maids and returned home at harvest time to help with the harvest. The patriarchal family farming lifestyle common in Bohemia existed also in Germany. Thus, in the eyes of single Czech men, German women could also be competent housewives and work in the fields, unlike American women. A good housekeeper was essential to a farming operation, and, in the absence of Czech women, Czech men looked for German wives.[61]

Czech shopkeepers needed to speak only German to do their business.[62] However, Czechs hung on to their ancestral language and to their traditional social activities and associations longer than the Germans. Czech children learned English slowly and they talked Czech outside the school, but acculturated faster if they were forced by circumstances to mix with Irish and American children. By the turn of the century most second-generation Czechs were bilingual.

The frontier moved relentlessly westward. In the annual report of 1891 the government of the United States advertised in newspapers destined for the Czech lands only Nebraska, Kansas, and Iowa as having land for settlers.[63]

For those wanting to acquire land after the 1860s, Kansas was one of the last states to be settled by the Czechs. Approximately fifteen hundred Czech farmers were settled in Kansas in 1900.[64] Practically all the Czechs lived in small towns and country districts of northwestern and central Kansas.[65]

Following 1870, many Czechs came to the Dakota Territory.[66] Many who eventually settled in the eastern sections of North and South Dakota did not come directly from rural Bohemia, but rather from Czech immigrant communities in Chicago and other American cities. They were usually skilled workers with no experience in farming.[67] Some Czechs came from other midwestern states.

Large numbers of Czech settlers arrived in the Dakotas at the turn of the century. In 1910, there were 7,287 settlers whose mother tongue was Czech in North Dakota, and 9,943 in South Dakota.[68] In South Dakota, Czechs lived in small towns such as Tábor, Tyndall, Tripp, and Armour, all in the southeastern quadrant of the state. The western part of the state was suitable only for ranching—a venture that few Czechs were willing to start.

North Dakota also had a few settlements with Czech names in the southeastern part of the state. Towns with names such as

Bechyň, New Hradec, Písek, Praha (Prague), and Veseleyville leave no doubt what region (southern Bohemia) the Czech immigrants left. According to one recent study of ethnic groups in North Dakota, "the Czechs have shown a predisposition to move into a city or town environment and take up urban occupations."[69] It is surprising that many early arrivals did not take up farming because that is the pattern everywhere else on the Great Plains, but it is entirely possible, even quite likely, that for those who left urban-industrial places like Chicago and had little first-hand knowledge of farming, the prospect of establishing a family-owned business in a small community with a concentration of Czechs was an attractive alternative to living in a big city and working in a dirty factory.

V. F. Kucera, his father (F. J.), mother (Marie), and aunt (Josephine). Kucera was born in Jarov, County Plzen, in 1859. He settled in Cheyenne County in 1885 and founded the Czech colony around Lodge Pole. Photo courtesy of Nebraska State Historical Society.

Chapter 5

 The Czechs in Nebraska

Influx of Czechs

Following the passage of the Homestead Act of 1862 (effective January 1, 1863), which made public lands available for a small registration fee, Czechs from east of the Missouri River and from Europe began arriving in growing numbers. The first Czech settlements followed the Missouri River. Completion of the railroad accelerated the influx, with the highest intensity of Czech immigration occurring in the 1880s.

Czech immigration had a rural character: Czechs and Moravians left villages and settled in small towns in rural communities. Only 17.6 percent lived in cities with a population of more than 25,000 in 1850–1900.[1]

What significance did the emigration to Nebraska play in the emigration from the Czech lands to the United States? In 1850 a mere five hundred immigrants had arrived on the shores of the New World. By 1900 the number had swelled to 200,000, out of which 8 percent (16,138) were settled in Nebraska.[2]

With the opening of Nebraska (which joined the union in 1867) to settlers, Czechs and Moravians immigrated in increasing numbers. The most dramatic increase occurred during the decade 1880–1890 when the Czech population in Nebraska doubled.

Selected Ethnic Groups Present in Nebraska, 1860–1880							
	1860	%	1870	%	1880	%	
Germany	1,742	27%	10,954	36%	31,125	32%	
Sweden	70	1%	2,352	8%	10,164	15%	
Norway	-	-	506	2%	2,010	2%	
Bohemia	-	-	1,770	6%	8,858	9%	
Austria	-	-	299	1%	2,346	2%	
total foreign-born	6,351		30,748		97,414		
total	28,826		122,993		452,400		
	1890	%	1900	%			
Germany	72,000	35%	65,506	37%			
Sweden	28,364	14%	24,693	14%			
Norway	3,632	2%	2,883	2%			
Bohemia	16,803	8%	16,138	9%			
Austria	4,032	2%	3,893	2%			
total foreign-born	202,542		178,030				
total	1,058,910		1,056,526				

Note: The relative numbers give the percentages of each ethnic group from the total foreign-born.

Source: Contribution of Population by leading countries (United States, Eighth Census, *Population*, 560, Ninth Census, *Population and Social Statistics*, 457, Tenth Census, *Population*, 492.

The table also shows that the proportion of the Czech and Moravian population in Nebraska to all foreign-born immigrants remained steady, as was also the case for the Norwegian, Swedish, and German populations between 1880 and 1900. In absolute numbers, however, the Czech and Moravian settlements experienced a tremendous growth between 1870 and 1890.[3] In 1890, Nebraska had a total of 202,542 foreign-born residents, of which 16,803 were Czech or Moravian (8.3 percent). Immigrants from the

Czech lands amounted to a significant portion of the total population, although the Swedes, for instance, outnumbered the Czechs by more than ten thousand (28,364).[4] By 1900, the number of people of foreign parentage in Nebraska was 178,030; of this number, 38,471 (21.6 percent) were from the Czech lands, with either both parents or one parent born in Bohemia or Moravia.[5]

During the last three decades of the nineteenth century Czechs and Moravians literally poured into Nebraska. Yet they were by no means the largest group. For example, if one were to list the top ten most populous Nebraska counties between 1860 and 1880, those with large Czech populations—with the exception of Douglas County (Omaha)—would not appear on such a table.

Czech settlement in Nebraska experienced rapid growth between 1870 and 1890, with a period of stabilization and a slight decrease by the end of the nineteenth century. The highest concentration of Czechs in Nebraska was in eastern counties; Butler, Saunders, Colfax, and Howard near the Platte River; Knox further north, and Saline County southwest of Lincoln. By the turn of the century, they dominated the foreign-born population in Saline and Colfax Counties, and were almost half of the foreign population in Butler County.

Douglas County stands apart from this analysis of rural settlements because most of the Czech population there lived in Omaha. In the 1880s and 1890s, Omaha Czechs experienced a tremendous growth in population. Omaha seemed to be the only urban "attraction" for Czech immigrants, who tended to settle on farms, often in remote and sparsely populated parts of Nebraska on the edge of the frontier, rather than in large towns.[6] In 1885 there were 10,163 Czech families in fifty-nine counties, one-tenth of them lived in Omaha.[7]

The total size of the Czech and Moravian population in the seven counties was 75.8 percent of all the immigrants from Czech lands residing in Nebraska in 1880. The total Czech and Moravian population between 1880 and 1890 grew, while the population of Saunders and Saline Counties stabilized. Butler, Colfax, and other counties in Nebraska experienced an accelerated growth as immigrants progressed to the West. The history of Skull Precinct illustrates the rapid influx of Czech settlers into Butler County. In 1870, Skull Precinct had fifty-nine Czechs; in 1895, the number rose ten-fold to nearly 500.[8] On June 22, 1878, a letter sent from Appleton in Butler County to *Pokrok Západu*, a newspaper published in Omaha since 1871, stated that 550 Czech and Moravian families had already settled in Butler County. The writer observed that Moravians almost exclusively settled an area between David City and Appleton. The Czechs and Moravians also settled an area along the Butler-Saunders County border, and then in Linwood, which was a spillover from Saunders County—an "older" Czech settlement where all the land was taken. In order to be close to other Moravians the newcomers settled the eastern part of Butler County.[9]

By 1900, the seven "old" Czech counties were well inside the demographic frontier, amounting to "only" 64.1 percent of the Czech population. The number of Czech settlers in the central and western counties grew at the expense of the growth of the eastern counties as the Czech population in Nebraska stabilized. This was most likely due to the good-quality land in the eastern counties being taken up; an important factor in the overall pattern of settlement. The proportion of Czechs to the total Nebraska population, with the exception of Omaha, declined by 1900.

The long journey to Nebraska

An analysis of the population schedules of the 1885 Federal Census of Nebraska reveals that the average Czech who came to Nebraska had tried states east of the Missouri and the Mississippi rivers. Czechs frequently stopped in Ohio and Minnesota before finally coming to Nebraska. Niles Carpenter, in *Immigrants and Their Children*, supported this idea when he described Czechs moving and settling in blocks of states. He considered it a typical phenomenon among Czechs anywhere in the Union. Carpenter described the Czech settlement patterns as a chain of states starting in New York and Pennsylvania and ending in the Midwest. Czech and Moravian paths to Texas were different; those settlers had known their destination before they left Europe, and a majority of them went from home directly to Texas without any stops in between. Thus, "most of the Texans had been more or less directly transplanted from their Moravian (or eastern Bohemian borderland) villages with a minimum disruption."[10]

The "1885 Nebraska Census" manuscript data listing birth places of children of immigrants offer an accurate picture of the passages across the American continent. This method assumes that the parents of the newborns lived in a given state when the mother delivered the child. In order to generalize about the movements of the ethnic groups following their arrival in the United States, it would be necessary to examine all the immigrant children's birth places.

The birth places of children born to a sample of immigrants from six precincts in Saunders and one from Saline Counties were used to examine the passages the immigrants followed. The data showed that Moravians chose the direct route to Nebraska.[11] The Czechs and the Swedes in the sample chose passages similar to each other but differed from the routes followed by Moravians. Their strategies or their circumstances were probably similar although the choice of the states they went through was not the same. Swedes were more likely than Czechs to take a northern route to Nebraska.

Although Iowa became a temporary home for both ethnic groups, almost half of the Swedes had stayed in Illinois, then continued westward, while only 18 percent of Czechs made the same decision. Many Czechs stopped in Wisconsin, while only 3 percent of the Swedes did so. Minnesota is probably an example of a state through which the two ethnic groups did not pass but, rather, stayed and settled. For many Czechs, Illinois (Chicago) had the same magnetic power.

This examination assumes that every stop that the immigrants made meant they tried different areas, or that they did not have any pre-set destination. The indirect routes could also indicate a migration of propertied immigrants, as most likely nobody else paid their way for them, and thus, nobody directed their routes. Those immigrants who went directly without stopping to one particular county or township might have followed their relatives or friends—they knew where they were going.

Emigration and target areas

Through a careful examination of the data collected by Frank Mareš and published in the first three volumes of the Czech newspaper, *Hospodář* (*The Farmer*), it is possible to delineate the emigration regions in Bohemia and Moravia and the target areas in Nebraska. The data appeared in *Hospodář* from March 1891 to May 1894 and again from March 1895 to September 1895.[12]

Generally, Czech emigration flowed from a geographically diverse area, as was the case of Swedish and Norwegian migration, although certain regularity of flow existed on a district level. Two counties, Saline and Saunders, are examples. Nearly all Czech immigrants to Saline County originated from southwestern and southern Bohemia. In stark contrast, nearly all the "Czechs" in Saunders County originated from southwestern Moravia.

In the case of the Czech and Moravian migration, there is only scant evidence of any "concentration of an immigrant population of homogeneous origins in a given locality," a definition Walter D. Kamphoefner uses to describe a chain migration.[13] ("Chain migration" refers to a phenomenon in which the first people from a particular village or district to emigrate are followed by relatives and friends; where this occurs there are clear links connecting many or most members of a particular ethnic group in a given locale in the New World.)

The previous chapter examined the personal reasons for emigration of Czechs from the Tábor and Písek districts. From the requests for permission to leave it is apparent that the applicants were heading to rural areas and often left because other members of their families or friends had left at an earlier stage. The requests do not give precise destination other than "America." Thus, it is possible only to establish that a great majority of immigrants from the Tábor and Písek Districts settled in Saline and Colfax Counties. Direct linkages based on names of migrants were successful only in a few cases.

The data from Mareš' survey of Czechs who settled in Nebraska in 1895 permits an examination of Czech migration on a village level. This data suggests that Czech immigrants who ended up in one county—namely, Saunders County—left from many different villages in one district in the Czech lands, rather than from a single village.

The small village of Litavany, in the Hrotovice district in the foothills of the Czech-Moravian Highlands, illustrates this point. In 1870, Litavany had sixty houses and 376 inhabitants. Arriving in Saunders County, two persons from Litavany went to the Chapman Precinct, two to Wahoo, four to Chester Precinct and three to Newman Precinct. If the focus of our observation is widened to include neighboring counties in Nebraska, we find only one or two families from Litavany in Butler County and three in Colfax County.[14]

Another example of a diffuse character of Czech migratory patterns on a village level is from a region east of Prague. A chronicle of a small village named Kluky, in the Kutná Hora region, showed that no fewer than half of the households left for the United States. The names from Kluky's chronicle were compared to the names of Czechs who had settled in Nebraska by 1892. One person, or possibly a family, settled in Butler County. (The chronicle unfortunately did not give the dates of departure of emigrants from Kluky.) The Kluky emigrant who came to Nebraska obviously did not follow others; nor did others follow him. Other village chronicles from the Kutná Hora region, compared to Mareš' data on Czech settlers in Nebraska, also revealed that only individuals or individual families reached Nebraska. If Nebraska is indicative of patterns in other states, Czechs often went their own separate ways upon arriving in the New World.[15]

Litavany and Kluky are typical of other villages in rural Bohemia and Moravia. Indeed, a close examination of the data leads to the conclusion that families from the same village in the Czech lands generally did not settle together in Nebraska. However, families in the same district in the Czech lands did tend to settle in the same county. Thus, if the geographic focus is widened from village to district (similar to a county), then at least a weak clustering pattern does become apparent.

In other words, some regularity in migratory patterns is observable. Czechs and Moravians from a particular region tended to emigrate to certain counties in Nebraska. Moravians from the Třebíč district dominated the "Czech" settlement of Saunders County and neighboring Butler County after 1867, settling in Plzeň and in Wahoo.[16] Moravians from the villages surrounding the towns of Třebíč, Brno-venkov (rural outskirts of Brno), and Znojmo, and Czechs from the Kutná Hora and the Havlíčkův Brod region (southeast of Prague), settled in Butler County. Czechs from the regions of Chrudim, Havlíčkův Brod, and Svitavy, and Moravians from the Třebíc and the Žďár nad Sázavou regions, settled in Colfax County in the late 1860s.[17]

Czechs who came to Saline County in 1865 left clusters of satellite villages that fell within the orbit of certain Bohemian towns, especially Domažlice, Klatovy, Jindřichův Hradec, Tábor, and Písek, all of which are located in southwestern and southern Bohemia. Immigrants to Saline County came also from the Rychnov nad

Kněžnou region in northeastern Bohemia and from the Mělník and the Kladno regions in central Bohemia, settling around Crete and Wilber after 1870.

The complex flows from the regions of Bohemia to Saline County reveal at least one anomaly: for some unknown reason, Bohemians from the Kutná Hora region, an area southeast of Prague, avoided Saline County like the plague. It is also noteworthy that only a few Moravians settled in Saline County.[18] Individual recollections point to the existence of a limited family network, and examples of some limited clustering of settlers from a particular area in Bohemia-Moravia in a specific locale in Nebraska did exist. For example, the immigrants from the Kutná Hora region dominated Howard County, while those from the Nymburk region dominated Knox County.

On a village level, however, emigration was geographically heterogeneous. Villages were not transplanted. Place names such as Prague and Bruno (Brno) used for the Czech settlements do not indicate the places of origins but rather a sentimental attachment to the large urban centers in the mother country.

The tendency for clustering appears to have been higher for Moravians than Bohemians. The Moravian emigration pockets were concentrated in small geographical areas. For example, about ten villages in the vicinity of Hrotovice, mentioned above, supplied a significant portion of the people who settled in the Chapman and Elk Precincts of Saunders County. Chapman Precinct had a total of eighty-three Czech-Moravian households in 1895, of which twenty-four came from the Hrotovice area. Moravians followed a direct route from the East Coast port cities to Nebraska, as if they knew their destination. This fact suggests that a degree of chain migration probably occurred in the case of Moravians. So, although certain areas in the Czech lands were caught up in emigration fever, no villages were transplanted.

Socio-economically, the relatively low number of families arriving together indicates emigration from the lower and middle social strata. Families at home waited until funds were forthcoming from members in the United States, enabling them to pay for their passage.[19] Unfortunately, the lack of data makes it impossible to employ the time factor into a useful analysis of the structure of immigrant groups (i.e., number of family members and gender).

Still, despite the economic hardships associated with emigration for many "third-wave" (later) Czech emigrants, Czechs (like Scandinavians and Dutch) were not paupers. They brought with them $23.12 per person in 1902, compared to an average for all other immigrants of $14.84.[20] This amount of money, while far from munificent, was significant because it enabled Czech immigrants to buy railroad tickets directly upon arrival in the ports of New York, Boston, Baltimore, and the like. It also gave them a little cushion on which to survive during the first difficult weeks and months on the frontier.[21]

Why Nebraska? How Czechs discovered the West

Czechs found out about Nebraska through articles and advertisements in newspapers, steamship lines, railroads, state emigration bureaus, colonizing groups, and individual letters which, taken together, produced abundant although not always accurate information about Nebraska. Railroad land agents and newspapers worked together in advertising Nebraska for settlement. The most notorious land speculator, an insurance agent in Omaha, was Václav L. Vodička, who came from Bohemia in 1868.

Vodička was born in Těchonice in southwest Bohemia. In Vienna he became a carpenter and gained experience in business. Later he recalled the patronizing attitude of Viennese towards Czechs, whom they often referred to as "Czech dogs."[22] In 1865 he arrived in Baltimore, stayed there for over a year, and then continued on to Ohio because he had been told by his German friends that the salaries were high. Vodička soon discovered the opportunities awaiting land agents in the newly opened Midwest, and decided to move to Omaha. He worked both as a land agent and as a member of the editorial staff of *Pokrok Západu* from 1877 to 1885.[23]

In 1875, the Slovania Colonization Club in Omaha organized a Czech settlement in Howard County, attracting mainly Minnesota Czechs who came originally from the region of Kutná Hora.[24] A settlement of about three hundred Czechs on the Niobrara River in Knox County was also a result of colonization efforts by Česká Osada (Czech Settlement), an organization of about five hundred members based in Chicago.[25] The underlying idea behind this effort was to establish a large Czech settlement on free land and to perpetuate the Czech language and Czech cultural awareness in the New

World. These Czechs came from the town of Sadská in the Nymburk region and settled mainly in Bohemia, Jefferson, and Niobrara townships.[26]

As noted earlier, individual letters helped to lure Czechs to Nebraska, although these letters often contained mixed signals, as Czech ethnographer Antonín Robek pointed out in 1984 in an article in *Český lid* (*Czech Nation*).[27] Robek suggested that relatives and friends who made the crossing often tried to persuade others to follow their lead, while at the same time sharing the sadness, homesickness, and hardships associated with doing so.[28] Thus, letters from America, in some cases, may have discouraged Czechs from going to the United States or Nebraska (or both).

Letters, newspapers, and agents promoting Nebraska emphasized the availability of cheap land—Nebraska's prime attraction. In the 1860s the press painted a rosy picture of the opportunities offered by homesteads on the Great Plains. However, many Czech settlers came to realize that homesteading was not without its drawbacks. The land was often of an inferior quality. Further, because the federal government had given railroads a significant amount of the best land, homesteaders were forced "to locate many miles remote from the right of way which had a disadvantage of long hauls over bad roads."[29]

Chapter 6

 A Dream Fulfilled: From
Peasants to Farmers

How did the Czech peasant-farmer cope with the unfamiliar conditions encountered in the Midwest? Did he transplant farming techniques and practices from the old country? The exigencies of frontier life—self-reliance, isolation, extreme weather, and the monoculture (corn growing)—were only a few of the challenges Czechs faced. Czechs came from villages; some of them re-entered into farming, but some had no experience in agriculture prior to their settlement in the Midwest.

The Czech response was to make a virtue out of necessity and develop strategies for getting started in farming. They assimilated into the success-oriented society with materialistic values. Their assimilation was based on two seemingly contradictory aspects: adaptability, and ideas and traditions carried over from the Old Country. Czechs were adaptable to the new conditions on the frontier; they succeeded by risk avoidance—a traditional fear of getting into debt—which they expressed in many ways. The most striking was their multi-crop strategy.

According to the findings of the Dillingham Commission, the Bohemians diversified in agriculture when they settled in rural regions, and the commissioners concluded that

> [Czechs were] thoroughly imbued with the progressive spirit of the West. They stand on the same social and economic plane as the better farmers in the

> community of whatever race, and in the second genera-
> tion are no longer foreign.[1]

The Commission grouped them together with Scandinavian and
German farmers; in terms of education and social status, the Commission considered them to be above the other Slavic races, who
were generally held to be inferior to "northwestern Europeans."[2]

The Czech immigrants were lured into the Midwest by the
free governmental land but when they arrived most of it was gone,
and the land had to be purchased from the railroads. This disillusionment was only one problem with which the settlers had to deal. How
well and how quickly did they adjust to the new environment? D.
Aidan McQuillan in *Prevailing Over Time*, the most recent and
comprehensive study of ethnic groups' adaptation to a new environment in a rural setting, measured ethnic success in terms of "risk
minimization."[3] Each farmer had to plan what crops to grow, had to
decide the size of an acreage under each crop, and had to decide how
much livestock and what kind to buy. The census manuscript data
tell the story of how successful these decisions were. Aggregate
numbers for each ethnic group show the degree of "Americanization"—adjustment of their value system to an American environment, which meant realization of the American Dream (i.e., material
success and independence).[4]

McQuillan studied three groups in central Kansas: Swedes,
Mennonites, and French Canadians. The present analysis focuses
on Czechs and Moravians in Nebraska.

Few Czechs came early enough to take advantage of the land
available through the Homestead Act of 1862. Even at this early
date, land in Nebraska was not "free." Allan G. Bogue, in *Money at
Interest*, argues that the term "free land" had been "used in promis-
cuous fashion." The land was never really up for grabs, since "some
10,690,990 acres of the 48,636,800 acres of Nebraska were claimed
by four railroads and the state government. These agencies disposed
of their holdings as profitably as possible." By 1870, they disposed
of almost one-third of Nebraska without "a recourse to the homestead law."[5] By 1878, no governmental land was left in any of the
state's eastern counties.[6]

Starting a farm was a costly undertaking and involved a great
deal more than the purchase of a piece of land. The cost of farming
varied over time. Location was also a major factor. At the height of
Czech immigration in the 1880s, a prospective farmer had to have

between $400 and $1,000 to get started.[7] For a farmer in Valley County in 1889, an estimated $900 was the minimum start-up cost; it was $400 in Hays County; and $600–$1,000 in Buffalo and Boone Counties.[8] The profits in the first three years were small: a "farmer could barely survive," wrote an observer from Howard County.[9]

Generally, Czechs were preoccupied with economic security. Most Czechs worked in Omaha or other Czech communities long enough to earn and save sufficient funds to buy farmland of their own. In a micro-study of one Czech community in Nebraska, Robert I. Kutak found that Czech immigrants did not like borrowing money for "unproductive purposes" and for "permanent things of life . . . everything ought to be based on cash basis."[10] Personal documents indicate that Czech farmers bridled at interest rates of 10–17 percent at the height of the Czech influx in the 1880s. Actually, interest rates had come down dramatically from the usurious (36 percent!) levels of the 1850s. Czechs, however, rarely borrowed money for the purchase of land or equipment. Fear of getting into debt permeates the letters of farmers. "I know some who even after twenty years in farming are still in debt," was the familiar lament of an older settler to newcomers.[11]

A Czech farmer, as other immigrants, used his savings from the home country to pay for the transportation to the Midwest. The money he brought with him rarely sufficed to set up a farm operation.[12] Rapidly rising land values lent a certain urgency to acquiring property at the earliest possible time. One farmer recalled in 1886:

> [When] I came I could not communicate with anybody. I dug two acres of sod and earned money in town to buy animals and two years later I started working my land.[13]

In the same year, another Czech farmer remembered the difficult start in Nebraska in 1869, when he arrived almost penniless:

> When I came to Omaha I bought eighty acres of land and had only three-and-half dollars left. Having worked in Omaha for six months I then moved to my property which is about seventy miles from Omaha [Dodge County—ed.], with fifteen dollars in cash. For four years I worked with no animals to pull the plow . . . To support my wife and two children I looked elsewhere for a livelihood.[14]

Twenty years later he took pride in the fact that his farm was valued at ten thousand dollars.

Sod house of Rudolph Zajicek family in 1884 in Webster County, Nebraska. Photo courtesy of Nebraska State Historical Society.

The early settlers received the land when it was free or bought it from railroads for a price that was initially low. Most of these early settlers had no intention of farming. Many people bought land for speculation or lived in cities and were rarely prepared to brave the often harsh conditions of the frontier beyond Omaha.[15] The reputedly hard-drinking Irish often sold out to the hard-working Czech farmers, according to a study of Czechs in Colfax County.[16]

Their pre-emigration experience equipped some Czech and Moravian immigrants with some knowledge of farming, but the many cooks, bookbinders, and shopkeepers, to name but a few others, had no background in agriculture.[17] "I am not ashamed of my temporary failure when I realize that I had never farmed before . . . and that I had only worked with a pen and books," wrote Czech immigrant Štědrý in 1891.[18] The passages many Czechs followed before they arrived in Nebraska indicate that some probably farmed in Ohio, Illinois, Wisconsin, and Minnesota, and thus gained some knowledge of American farming.

A Czech farmer did not need to be able to speak the English language to be successful, but the inability to speak it was a barrier even in rural areas, and Czechs, as other ethnic groups, solved it in their own way. In Omaha and in the small communities Czechs strove to be self-sufficient in their services. For example, Czech businesses sprang up even where it meant duplicating already existing German or American enterprises. Czechs preferred to patronize stores run by Czech-speaking proprietors; they thought that a Czech grocer or butcher would cater to their needs better than one who did not speak their language. Take the small town of Verdigre, Knox County, for example. The town had both German and Czech grocers, two saloons, and two restaurants, one English and one Czech. There were also German and Czech butchers.[19] *Pokrok Západu* frequently printed letters asking for a Czech doctor, an ironmonger, or a cooper "since so far we have only one but he is an American."[20] For example, F. J. Vávra, from Valley County, advertised in 1882 for a Czech cooper to come to "this large settlement" (St. Paul). Vávra had a "place for him in the County and he will give him a piece of land."[21] Such pleas reflected the same desire—to have someone with whom Czechs could communicate and who could understand their needs.

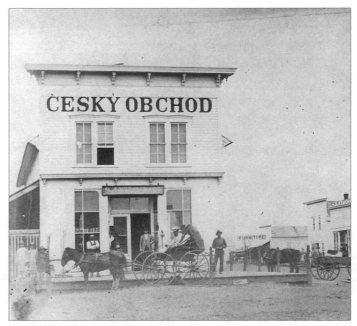

Wilber, Nebraska, in 1875. Cesky Obchod means Czech grocery store. Photo courtesy of Nebraska State Historical Society.

Above: The Jacob S. Hunt loghouse completed in 1864 (first loghouse in the Wilber area). Below: Emma Kral at left in Swanton, Nebraska, about 1889 (immigrated from Bohemia in 1878). Photos courtesy of Nebraska State Historical Society.

Frontier farmers: Czechs in the rural Midwest

Most of the Czech and Moravian immigrants came from social groups of the *sedlák* (farmer) who had 25–200 acres and a farmhouse, and the *chalupník* or *malorolník* (cottager) who owned 5–25 acres and a small cottage. In the Midwest these peasants had to get accustomed to working on a much larger space.[22] An average farm in the United States was 160 acres, a size which made farm machinery essential.[23]

Czech farmers were thrifty and they tended to rely on their own networks rather than invest money into expensive farming equipment. Many Czech farmers borrowed a plough from a neighbor and reciprocated by working off the "debt" or payment in kind.[24] Neighbors lending or borrowing equipment and helping each other were elements of traditional village life that were brought from the old country. The stories told by settlers of getting together for thrashing and harvesting described events similar to the annual village fairs in the Old World. "Harvesting was a family affair—all the males from a family, neighbors and cousins got together, loaded bundles pitching them into the threshing machine," according to one source. "Women prepared food, children played games, and everybody gathered in the evening at home to drink home brew."[25]

Young Czech farmers were inexperienced with farming on the Great Plains, but many relied on advice from their fathers—a tradition from the Old Country. Few fathers knew that on the Plains, to reap good harvests over a long period of time, they had to plow deep into the ground to reach the subsoil moisture.[26]

In Nebraska Czech farmers hired laborers, according to data based on U.S. Census of 1885. The American version of *čeledín*—a hired hand in the Czech lands—received sixteen to twenty dollars per week, and a maid two to three dollars including board, an expense for which some Czech farmers were prepared to budget.[27] Czech farmers who hired laborers typically hired Czech persons.[28]

Children also worked with their fathers, or a farmer hired his relatives for room and board in exchange for domestic help or farm work. Parents, particularly mothers-in-law, helped in the household as "maids" or "servants," according to the U.S. Census records. Wives and daughters did housework, but a passerby would not generally see women working in the fields, except at harvest time, as much as they had done in the home country.[29] Milking a cow, for example, became a man's domain in the United States—a chore men would have been ashamed to do in the Old Country.[30]

As mentioned above, many Czechs could not afford to buy a farm immediately. Those who had insufficient funds or did not want to work in town often became tenant farmers. Tenants could either receive one-third of the harvest or a set sum of money based on the number of acres they farmed. Some young men simply stayed on the family farm and eventually took over when their parents retired. A few Czech tenant farmers owed their landlessness to mismanagement and lack of thrift.[31]

Many Czech settlers bided their time and bought out Irish settlers and American farmers. Americans normally sold their land cheaply, according to a Czech farmer, who thought that Americans wanted to move "at least once a year since it runs in their blood, . . . and because they are surrounded by Czechs."[32]

Another sign of the Czechs' careful approach to farming was their strategy of growing a variety of crops. This plan required substantial "up front" costs, but protected Czech farmers against a crop failure or a low market price for a single commodity. The agricultural schedules in U.S. Census manuscript from 1885 offer the most accurate picture of the crop diversification. They show that the immigrants from the Czech lands followed a strategy of the highest crop diversification in comparison to other ethnic groups. Moravians particularly stand out with their average of four crops for an individual farmer. Further statistical analysis proved that each other country of origin had a statistically smaller mean crop diversity than Moravia.

According to U.S. Census records, between 1860 and 1880 the most common combination of crops grown by Czechs was corn, wheat, oats, potatoes, and barley.[33] In 1889, almost the same pattern still held: corn, wheat, oats, rye, and barley.[34] Potatoes, flax, buckwheat, and vegetables were also among the staples.

Flax, the "Czech and Moravian" crop used for the production of linen and also as a fodder, was not well suited for the semi-arid soils of Nebraska. Peasants grew flax for fiber in Bohemia and Moravia, in Nebraska they grew it for seed.[35] Czech farmers continued growing flax despite the extreme Nebraska summers unsuitable for this crop. This crop brought higher yields than the best wheat, but demanded more labor.[36]

In the last decade of the nineteenth century the immigrants accommodated to the needs of the market and fully accepted the "American" crop—corn. In 1889, Czech farmer Josef Novotny explained his own decision to grow corn in the following way:

> . . . my neighbors decided to sow wheat in the spring, I have decided not to sow any. The price of wheat is better than last year, but when I think of all the machinery, debt and work involved with growing it? Corn is easy to grow, I shall harvest it with my children and I shall clean it myself, too.[37]

Czech farmers realized that corn provided better yields in the Midwestern climate than wheat, a crop with which they were familiar.[38] The blizzard of 1891 brought many Czech farmers to the brink of bankruptcy:

> We would have gone bankrupt even in heaven if we farmed the same way we do here [in Sheridan County]. All of us wanted to have as much land as possible. We came and plowed our land, but only two inches deep; we sowed corn, marrow, melon and had a good harvest. In the second year, we added wheat and oats, and again the harvest was good. We plowed in the third year, and sowed again. We did not have enough farming machinery, so we bought it on credit. In the fourth year, we sowed all we could. So far all was fine. We yielded 25–35 bushels of wheat per acre, and sold it for forty cents a bushel; later on in the year we received eighty cents and in the spring one dollar. After the harvest, the mortgage needed to be paid off but in the following year we had a bad harvest and the banks loaned money for forty percent interest. A disaster was bound to happen. We are originally townsfolk and we had hoped that koláče would grow on trees [in America].[39] We cannot buy anything because we have no money; we cannot borrow because all our land is mortgaged. Our children are small and we cannot even send them to school, nor can we feed them.[40]

Taking risks, something the Czechs did not like to do, was necessary for survival in the West. Switching to ranching was one answer to recurring difficulties in farming. In 1889, for example, a Czech settler in Nebraska claimed that raising cattle was more profitable than farming. "If a rancher has one hundred to two hundred head of cattle his livelihood is more secure than that of a rich farmer since the former can sell off his three year old cattle for thirty dollars a piece."[41] Only a few die-hard Czechs persevered in western Nebraska; many returned to the eastern counties or left the state.

Chapter 7

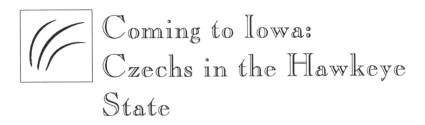

Coming to Iowa: Czechs in the Hawkeye State

When they first arrived in Iowa in the early 1850s, shortly after Iowa had become a state (December 28, 1846), the Czech pioneers often recorded their first impressions of life on the prairie in letters to family and friends in the Old Country. In a letter dated December 26, 1863, written to his relatives in Litomyšl, Bohemia, Josef Kostlán, who settled in Linn County, described the immensity of the New World (all of Europe could move to America and the population density would still be less); the wildlife (few deer, but many small animals like rabbits and pheasants); the availability of land (very abundant compared to the Old Country); the cost of living (cattle are expensive); the absence of social classes on the frontier (rich and poor are respected equally); economic and political rights (one can recover lost property through hard work and no one is afraid to express his opinion publicly); and human dignity (in America, people do not carry heavy burdens on their own shoulders, they have animals for that purpose). He also expressed surprise that cattle were kept outside throughout the year and that only the horses stayed in barns in the winter. Burning forests to gain more arable land was another practice the newcomer had not seen before. The weather seemed quite extreme, particularly the winds because there are no mountains in Iowa.[1]

Often Czech pioneers like Josef Kostlán added passing comments about items that might seem mundane to a serious reader, such as the differences in clothing. For example, Kostlán mentioned that women wore long dresses and caps or hats. A woman can get a job in town and "all she has to do is laundry and clean the house." Nonetheless, Kostlán did not think that life was much better for women in America than in Bohemia, since they were isolated and lonely.[2]

Reading between the lines, it is evident that language was a barrier to be overcome. For example, Kostlán noted that English-Americans were sincere and good-natured people as long as one could communicate with them. Another barrier—not unrelated to problems of communication among the ethnically diverse new arrivals on the ever-receding frontier—was loneliness. Sometimes this longing for the Old Country permeated every sentence of letters home; other times due to pioneer pride or Bohemian diffidence, it was necessary, again, to read between the lines. But the homesickness was almost always there, like hay fever at harvest time or a recurring attack of rheumatism. Only the aching was not in the joints but in the heart—a pain no emolument could touch.

Why Iowa?

The fertile soil of Iowa was the biggest attraction of this midwestern state for the Czech settlers. When Wisconsin and Minnesota no longer had available or affordable land, Czech settlers headed south. Many urban-dwelling Czech-Americans from places like Chicago and Cleveland thought that as farmers they could be self-reliant. In the cities they often had worked in degrading jobs because the best jobs had already been taken by immigrants from Ireland and Germany who arrived ahead of them. Sometimes employment of any kind was scarce. The fact that many Czechs had large families was another reason why farming was attractive: if they could buy land the small children would have plenty of fresh air and wide open spaces to play in, and the older children would make good farm hands. They would learn the value of hard work and could take over when the parents grew old.

In 1852 the first Czechs, looking for cheap land, came from Racine and Caledonia, Wisconsin. The railroad beyond the Mississippi River had not been built at that time. They ferried across the river and continued by ox team to Johnson and Linn Counties.[3] Linn County and the northern part of Johnson County had permanent settlements already in 1854.[4]

Many Czech immigrants who came to Iowa in the last two decades of the nineteenth century responded to invitations from friends and relatives who had arrived in Iowa in the 1850s. Some had been recruited by agents of shipping companies and railroads who competed with one another to attract settlers to Iowa as to other midwestern states.

The frontier states also competed for immigrants because land sales and industrial development depended to a considerable degree on immigration. Indeed, the population problem these new western states faced in the early stages of their economic development was exactly the opposite of that facing many developing countries today: they were severely underpopulated rather than overpopulated. Iowa, for example, had a state immigration agency with a commissioner in New York. According to Marcus L. Hansen, "from 1870 to 1873, the State Board of Immigration not only published handbooks in several foreign languages, but sent agents to European ports to persuade foreigners to locate in Iowa. The State spent a total of $29,500 to encourage immigration."[5] Immigrants would not only till the land, they would build towns, start businesses, and pay taxes. Today immigrants are often seen as a burden; in the nineteenth century they were the key to winning the West.

The pioneers who settled in Iowa in the early 1850s, unlike those who came later, were prepared for life on the frontier; they brought seeds to plant in their gardens and fields, and tools to build their houses. They settled on the banks of the Iowa River in Johnson County.[6] But few of these pioneers had enough money to purchase land immediately, and thus many used the strategy of going to work on somebody else's farm. Although they were paid a living wage, farm hands could rarely save enough money to buy their own land in the first few years.

The majority of the Iowa settlers came in the second half of the nineteenth century. This influx of Czech immigrants peaked in the 1890s. By the turn of the century, all the free or cheap land near Czech settlements was taken and the rate of immigration declined. By that time, 10,809 foreign-born Czechs lived in Iowa.[7] These newcomers, in contrast to the early Czech settlers, were poor and brought "little more than the clothing they were wearing," and a lot of courage, according to Cyril Klimesh.[8] They were fortunate to find good land in Linn County (specifically, in College and Putnam Townships, north of Johnson County).[9] Klimesh suggested that the likeness of the landscape in this part of Iowa to the bucolic country-side of southern Bohemia softened the sense of separation and homesickness many Czechs experienced living on the prairie.[10]

Of farms and families

The case of František Švehla illustrates how important own-ing a farm was to the Czech settlers of Iowa. František Švehla, from southern Bohemia, came to Iowa in 1860 and settled in Winneshiek County. He worked for six years as a farm hand and saved as much money as he could. He eventually bought 280 acres of prairie land. Why had he been so eager to get land of his own? What had motivated him to make the trek to Iowa with little money? Why had he worked and saved for six long years for the chance to own a piece of ground that would only yield its fruits in return for backbreaking work, if at all? Simply, because "none else would benefit from this work and one can be twice as productive if one works for oneself."[11] Czech farmers as a whole had a low rate of tenancy—an indicator of stability suggesting that Czechs as a whole were content to stay put, bought their own property as soon as they could, and did not move for the sake of moving.

Most Czech settlers could not immediately afford to buy land even at low frontier prices. In the 1850s, it generally cost around $2,000 to start a farm in Iowa. According to Klimesh, Czech farmers "managed to get by with only a small fraction of this." However, even a "small fraction" of the average-sized farm in Iowa was likely to be a piece far greater that anything they could have afforded in the Old Country. Generally speaking, Czechs made do with less than other ethnic groups, including the English-Americans.[12] In Iowa as elsewhere, they made the American Dream come true through thrift, perseverance, and hard work, rather than by having anything handed to them on a silver platter. In this sense, Czech-Americans on the frontier exemplify the values and virtues, the sacrifices and exertions, on which that great continental empire, the United States of America, was built in the nineteenth century.

For Czech settlers in Iowa, farming was a way of life, not just another occupation. They had a close bond to the land. Like horses and carriages, families and farms went together. One was incomplete without the other. Thus, the family farm was the Czech-American Dream. In Bohemia, the rule was "once poor, always poor"; in America, anything was possible with hard work. That was a challenge the Czech settlers of Iowa eagerly accepted.

Czechs are sociable people. In the frontier days, as now, getting together with friends and relatives was important to them. Thus, many Czech farmers settled near Czech communities. The individualism of the frontier did not come naturally to Czechs, whose village-centered traditions emphasized communal and familial values rather than materialistic or individualistic pursuits (witness the importance of pubs, festivals, and the like in the everyday life of rural communities in Bohemia or Moravia).

Many early Czech settlers bought land in the vicinity of Cedar Rapids. By 1856, 139 Czechs had already settled there. By the turn of the century, Cedar Rapids was 20 percent Czech, making it the "most Czech" city in the United States, according to one source.[13] When František Kubela and his family arrived in the United States in 1864, they were homesick and longed to live among other Czech immigrants. They decided to go to Cedar Rapids, abandoning Cincinnati, Ohio, where the few Czechs who lived there apparently did not socialize with one another very much.[14]

When Czech settlers came to Cedar Rapids, they purchased land—usually forty acres—near the city. In Cedar Rapids as elsewhere, Czech settlers were motivated by a desire to leave a legacy of land and to pass along a way of life.[15] From the memoirs of the old settlers, however, it is also clear that parents were proud of the fact that they could give their progeny something they themselves had not had—material security in the form of land, farm buildings, and machinery.

As most Czechs arrived on the frontier without much money, everybody in the family had to contribute. Men either worked as hired hands, gaining valuable farm experience in the process, or worked at local mills, railroad construction sites, or wherever they could get a job. Older children often looked for work in towns, too, if they were not needed on the farm.[16] In the winter, women did laundry for city folk.[17] Women also contributed by doing things that saved money, for example, growing flax, spinning linen, and making clothing for the family.[18]

Pochobradsky's store in the Czech Village in Cedar Rapids, circa 1900. Photo courtesy of The National Czech & Slovak Museum & Library.

The Pochobradsky family in front of their store in Cedar Rapids, Iowa. Photo courtesy of The National Czech & Slovak Museum & Library.

The Pochobradsky family inside their store in the Czech Village. Photo courtesy of The National Czech & Slovak Museum & Library.

The term "sod-buster" did not come about by accident. The first challenge often facing a neophyte farmer on the frontier was to break virgin ground.* According to Josef Kostlán, a large steel plow of a kind Czechs had not seen in Europe was used for this purpose. It took five oxen to pull the plow efficiently. But plows were expensive and Czech farmers rarely had more than two oxen. Some had none. As a consequence, many early settlers were able to plow only a few acres a year.[19]

The poor harvests in the 1850s and 1860s reflected the risks and uncertainties frontier farmers faced. By 1870 the Czechs began to prosper.[20] Czech farmers, like other pioneers, wanted to be self-reliant. They grew wheat for the market, and planted potatoes, oats, and Indian corn for their own use. When bad weather and cinch bugs took a toll on wheat harvests around 1880, they had to look for another cash crop, and, as in Nebraska, they chose corn. [21]

---

*AUTHOR NOTE: The following description of the Czech pioneer farming is largely based on Cyril Klimesh's work, *They Came to This Place*.

Compared to Bohemia, the social geography of farming on the Iowa frontier was radically different. Czech immigrants came from villages where communal bonds were strong and where people lived "within easy talking distance."[22] On the vast midwestern plains, Czechs faced life in unprotected and isolated dwellings.[23]

Dvořák in Spillville

Antonín Dvořák, the famous Czech composer, visited Iowa in the summer of 1893. Dvořák and his family travelled by train to Spillville (Winneshiek County) for a four-month holiday. His observations on life in Spillville, a predominantly Czech community in northeast Iowa, document the loneliness that often stalked the early settlers. Dvořák was so impressed by the solitary existence of Czech families that he warned Czechs not to leave their country.

With a population of 361, Spillville Czechs came mostly from villages in eastern and southern Bohemia. Some came directly from the port of arrival and some stopped in cities east of the Mississippi River.[24] The first Czechs purchased federal or "school" land in the area around Spillville in 1854 (the proceeds from the sale of school land were to be used for the maintenance of the public school in the township).[25] When they left Bohemia, they planned to settle in Cleveland, Ohio, but upon arriving in the United States, they heard that government land was being sold in Iowa. So they headed west. To Spillville.[26]

By 1860, Czech settlements dominated Winneshiek County. That year, seventy-two Czech families lived in the county; the 1885 census showed 888 Czechs concentrated in the southwestern townships.[27] Eventually, Czechs outnumbered the original German and Swiss pioneers.[28] Klimesh observed that in Iowa the Czechs mixed with German neighbors but, as in Texas, tended to avoid associating with other ethnic groups.[29]

Dvořák came to Spillville on an invitation from a Prague acquaintance, one Jan Josef Kovařík (1850–1939), a viola and violin player with the New York Philharmonic and formerly a student of Prague Conservatory.[30] Young Jan Josef was one of the six children (all gifted musicians) of Jan Kovařík, a teacher, organist, and prominent member of the Spillville community. "Soon after the arrival of the first Czechs on land near the Turkey River, the settlers, despite their poverty, sent to southern Bohemia in 1869 for . . . Jan Kovařík [the elder]."[31]

Young Kovařík thought that Dvořák would feel right at home among the Czech settlers in Spillville. Kovařík also arranged for Dvořák to visit other Czech communities in Iowa, because he knew of the composer's homesickness.

In February 1893, Dvořák wrote that he "decided to stay in the United States" over the summer to get to know the country better.[32] Normally, he would have gone back to Bohemia for the summer, but he had a special project planned: the *Symphony in E minor (From the New World)*. He could not have written it if he had not stayed in the United States that summer, he later declared.[33] Many Dvořák admirers believe he wrote all or part of the "New World" symphony during his stay in Spillville, but there is still much controversy surrounding this question. What is not controversial is that Dvořák found Iowa musically inspirational. During the summer of 1893, he composed the *String Quartet in F Major*, which combined the sounds of the birds, fields, and prairies around Spillville, according to Klimesh. By the end of his stay in Iowa, Dvořák also finished the *String Quintet in E Flat*, a piece inspired by the dancing and drum beating of the Indians.[34] Moreover, Dvořák could hear the compositions immediately, since Spillville had plenty of local talent including the Kovařík family of musicians. Spillville's music lovers eagerly arranged a concert which could have been billed as the "world premier" of Dvořák's new compositions![35]

Before Dvořák left New York for Iowa, he had Kovařík tell him all about Spillville; he even asked him to draw a plan of the settlement. Spillville was a Catholic community. Father Bílý energetically administered St. Wenceslaus church from 1888 until 1894. The composer and the priest became fast friends. The church organ and Father Bílý's ponies were among the greatest attractions for Dvořák and his family. "Riding Father Bílý's ponies will be good for my children," an excited Dvořák wrote back to his friends in Bohemia.[36]

Surrounded by Czech farmers, Dvořák felt almost at home in Spillville. Dvořák was keenly interested in the personal histories and circumstances of Czechs who had immigrated to Iowa. What areas of Bohemia and Moravia had they left? When had they first arrived here? He went to Spillville cemetery, and, by looking at the gravestones, Dvořák found that most of the Czechs came in the

1850s, and were born in southern Bohemia around Písek, Tábor, and České Budějovice.[37]

Dvořák was impressed by the endurance of the Iowa Czechs. During his stay in Spillville, he walked every day along the Turkey River and often talked to the old settlers about their experiences in the New World. Farmers often lived miles apart. The sparseness of the population added to the sense of isolation many farmers felt, he concluded.[38] Despite the fact that the farmers did well in Iowa, Dvořák advised Czechs not to emigrate to the United States. "Now [in 1893] it is not as it used to be: the land is expensive and immigrants must go West where the land is free or cheap."[39] Furthermore, Dvořák found the climate less than agreeable. The weather was too hot and the prairies were like the Sahara.[40]

> [There is] nothing here but fields and meadows. That is all. There is never any person in sight as everybody rides. The cattle you see both in the summer and in the winter. Milking is done here by men. It is all wild here, sometimes so sad that a person could go quite mad here. Getting used to the conditions is the only way to survive here.[41]

Dvořák was dismayed when he realized that there was no brewing or sale of beer in Iowa. Drinking beer was for most Czechs an important part of life, liberty, and the pursuit of happiness. Imbibing was not frowned upon in Bohemia or in Czech communities in the Midwest. As long as a settler took good care of his farm, kept his fences mended and his animals healthy, he could get drunk and his neighbors would not be outraged. Parents in Bohemia (then and now) would think nothing of sending small children to an inn to fetch a pitcher of beer for the family.[42]

The state of Iowa prohibited the sale of liquor in 1855. Following the influx of German immigrants, the law was amended in 1858 to permit the manufacture and sale of beer. In the early pioneer period, a federal liquor license cost $25.[43] Klimesh suggested that every community that had both a German and Czech population could support at least one brewery.[44]

The early saloons resembled those from the Old World. They were sparsely furnished and the liquor was sold over a short counter and patrons sat on wooden benches. The saloons served an important social function for the farmers. People came to hear the latest news and to hunt for jobs.[45]

Prohibition in Iowa was resurrected in the 1880s.[46] Enforcement of the anti-liquor law created many convictions and arrests but, as Dvořák noticed, alcohol was sold in the taverns anyway despite the threat of a stiff fine if the proprietor was caught in the act. "Americans are strange," Dvořák wrote. "They like beer but they pass laws doing away with alcohol in Iowa." No wonder Dvořák decided "life is better at home!"[47]

Dvořák left Spillville on September 16, 1893, having spent three months he would always remember fondly. Among his fondest memories were playing a Czech card game, drinking with the townsfolk of Spillville, and riding horses with his family every day.[48] He saw the priest and played organ every day, too. Once he played at a Czech farm wedding.[49] He became quite popular with the grandmothers and grandfathers in the village because he played their favorite hymns.[50] He liked Iowa but he did not decide to spend a whole summer there because of its rustic charms: "If Czechs were not living there I would not have visited Spillville," he wrote upon his return to New York.[51]

As Spillville's most celebrated guest, Antonín Dvořák was struck by the contrast between the rich social life of Czech peasants in rural Bohemia where people typically lived in villages surrounded by friends and family and the solitary, lonely existence of Czech farmers in Iowa. Dvořák could empathize with these stout-hearted Czech-Americans because they spoke the same language, enjoyed the same food and drink, and felt homesick for the same "home"— like that of most Czech settlers in Iowa, Dvořák's home was a quiet village in the verdant countryside of Bohemia. But unlike his Czech hosts in Iowa, Dvořák was in the United States only temporarily— he knew he would soon return home. To Europe. To familiar sights and sounds and smells. To Bohemia. Many Czech settlers did not have this option. Some could not afford to go back for financial reasons, some had too much invested (and not only in a material sense). After all, the goal in coming to the United States in the first place was to achieve the Czech peasant's version of the American Dream—to own a farm and to raise a family in dignity and free of debt or indenture. This was a goal that seemed unattainable in Bohemia in the second half of the nineteenth century.

So they came to America. To Wisconsin, Minnesota, Iowa, and even beyond, to Nebraska and the Dakotas. They came to build a future for themselves and their children. Had they returned to

Bohemia, they would have had to admit defeat. And that is something they could not do. They were pioneers and they had an indomitable spirit. Without it they could not have survived in this brave new world. Farms are not portable and so neither was the future for these Czechs of Spillville. The same could be said of all the other Czech settlers in all the other "Spillvilles" that had sprouted in countless places across the Great Plains like clover patches in spring.

Dvořák was thoroughly Czech but he was different from the Czechs he encountered in Iowa. His future was portable. He could go anywhere in the world and prosper. He did not have to wonder what would become of his wife and children if he decided to move on. Nor did he have to worry that their future would suffer if he chose to stay put, or to come and go. And so he came to America and to Iowa to have a look, but he soon went home again, to his beloved village in Bohemia. That was a luxury the Czech settlers in Iowa and elsewhere did not have. But then, for the pioneers, luxury of any kind was out of the question.

Chapter 8

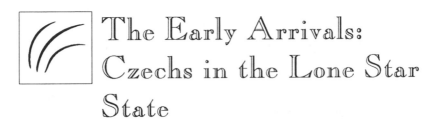 The Early Arrivals:
Czechs in the Lone Star
State

Texas is the only state in the South with a large Czech population. Totaling 750,000, Czech-Americans now make up about 5 percent of the population of Texas and, surprisingly, Czech was quite possibly the third most commonly spoken language in Texas (behind English and Spanish) as recently as 1983.[1]

Germans outnumbered Czechs during the heyday of European immigration in the nineteenth century but, unlike Czechs, Texas Germans in time gravitated to cities where they were assimilated and, being surrounded by people of varying ethnic backgrounds, found that English was the only functional language. Another reason why the German language almost died out was because Germany was America's enemy in both world wars and many German-Americans were ashamed and/or frightened of speaking German and even of having German ancestry. Any such inhibitions were less compelling for Czech-Americans.

The first Czech arrivals in Texas, fourteen in all, settled in Cat Spring in 1847, two years after Texas joined the Union following a bruising war with Mexico.[2] By 1870 there were approximately 1,000 Czech immigrants, mostly from Moravia, living in scattered communities. In the early 1860s, during the Civil War, immigration came to a virtual halt.[3] After the Civil War a new wave of immigration brought thousands more Czechs to Texas: the 1900 Census listed 9,204 foreign-born Czechs, and in 1910, when their numbers rose to over 15,000, Czechs were second only to Germans in population size.[4]

Letters from Texas

The pattern of Czech-Moravian immigration to Texas was unique. While the Czechs came to the Midwest from a belt covering a relatively large area of Bohemia and western Moravia, Czech-Texans came mostly from villages in northern Moravia (a few came from northeastern Bohemia). Many were from the area around Frenštát in northern Moravia. This type of immigration from villages within one district is a form of "chain migration" (the concentration of immigration from the same area in the old homeland into the same area in the new).[5] The importance of word-of-mouth information in this process is evident from the testimony of the newcomers themselves. In 1907 an old-timer remembered that in some areas in Moravia people did not hear about any other state but Texas.[6] Tomáš Hruška, a native of the Frenštát area who settled in Fayetteville, recalled that "in the fall of 1855 my parents with many other people from many villages . . . set out on a direct journey to Texas."[7] In other words, these Czechs, for whom the New World was only an abstract idea, were not going to "America" so much as they were going to Texas.

Many Czechs first heard about Texas after it achieved statehood in 1845. A gigantic expanse of territory compared to the Czech lands (five countries the size of modern day Czechoslovakia would fit into Texas, with room to spare), the fledgling state of Texas needed settlers. Like a giant sponge, there was practically no limit to how many newcomers Texas could absorb. Early Czech arrivals, among them one Reverend Josef A. Bergman, sent letters to the Old Country describing the great opportunities that awaited Czech immigrants to the new Lone Star State.[8] The timing of these letters could not have been more providential: they arrived in the late 1840s and early 1850s at a time when the peasants of Bohemia and Moravia were suffering through a series of bad harvests.

Respected and trusted leaders in the villages stimulated curiosity about this place called Texas by circulating these letters, a phenomenon rare in emigration of Czechs to other parts of the United States.[9] The *Moravské noviny* (*Moravian News*) also published a few of the Texas letters.[10] Typically, newspapers, like letters, were passed around—something which was natural in small villages where everybody knew everybody else and news about the world beyond the village gates was always something special. Those who were most eager to go, often the wealthy peasants who were leaders in the villages, encouraged others to join them.

Sometimes the "respected" leaders were not honest. František Branecký of Lišná, Moravia, wrote in his memoirs how the wealthy farmer F.P. deceived him. F.P. promised Branecký a "comfortable future." He would pay for Branecký's passage to America in return for which Branecký would work for F.P as a hired hand. Branecký, the youngest of six children, inherited very little; F.P. made him an offer he could not refuse. But once Branecký was in Texas, F.P. began backpedaling. At first he did not want to hire Branecký at all. Then, when he finally did, F.P. treated Branecký like a slave.[11] The significance of this story transcends the life of a single individual. The fact is that there were many Braneckýs in the saga of Czechs in America. The simple peasants who left the security of their quiet villages in the Czech countryside were often unprepared for the predatory methods of steamship and railroad agents, immigration officials, land speculators, and, yes, even their own compatriots, like F.P.

Letters were often enough to start a migration process, but there were times when other circumstances accelerated emigration. For example, when peasants in northern Moravia did not prosper economically in the 1870s, they became especially susceptible to emigration fever. The Austrian government, in an attempt to stop this epidemic of emigration, supported *internal* migration (that is, within the Austro-Hungarian Empire).

In the early 1870s, for instance, many people in northern Moravia considered migration to Banat, Hungary. Hungarians (or Magyars), a non-Slavic people, were not enthusiastic about the prospect of an influx of Slavs, a fact that must have discouraged the Czechs. The sound of the door to Hungary slamming shut made them all the more receptive to inducements from the New World. Following the Civil War, a spate of new letters from Texas Czechs informed friends and relatives back home that the guns had gone silent, the Union was preserved, and there was still cheap and fertile land available in Texas. The letters from the New World also emphasized that political and religious freedom were guaranteed in

America, something Czechs could not count on in Hungary (or, for that matter, under Austrian rule in Bohemia). The more they knew the more quickly their minds were made up.[12]

The highway to Texas

The way Czechs emigrated to Texas—the path they followed—was different from that of Czechs on the Great Plains. Generally speaking, these Czechs, as noted earlier, were going directly to Texas rather than to "America." Czech emigrants who eventually settled in Texas usually went via Bremen (rather than via Hamburg). In fact, studies and memoirs of Czech Texans indicate that "except for those who came to Texas from the Midwest, virtually all Czech Texans came this way."[13]

The ships from Bremen headed directly for Galveston in the Gulf of Mexico rather than Boston, New York, or Baltimore on the East Coast. The fact that Galveston was the primary port of debarkation leaves no doubt that the Texas Czechs knew exactly where they were going before they got on the boat. Had they boarded ships in Hamburg they might have landed at any one of several ports along the eastern seaboard (either in the United States or Canada). From these ports, they might have gone to Cleveland, Chicago, St. Louis, or Omaha. Or they might have joined a wagon train heading west. In other words, for many Czechs going to America the phrase "destination unknown" was apt. But not for the Czechs of Texas.

"Tex-Czechs"

This identical formative experience must have created a special feeling of belonging, of having had a common experience coming to America, for Czech-Texans, setting them apart from the rest of the Czech-Americans. If Texans are known for their strong sense of identity as Texans, there are good reasons for the Czech community in Texas to have a special sense of identity as "Tex-Czechs." The odyssey from Moravia to Cat Spring, a fateful journey not only from one continent to another but also from one world to another, created a kind of shared experience which set them apart.

But the "highway" from Moravia to Texas did not end in Galveston. Having arrived in Galveston, the immigrants usually took a schooner to Houston, where they stayed long enough to gather the supplies for the journey still ahead. The first settlers went to their final destination, Cat Spring in Austin County, either on foot or, together with children, supplies, and possessions, in ox-drawn wagons.[14] The time required to travel the distance between Houston and Cat Spring was twenty-one days by wagon. Later arrivals from the Czech lands would continue to travel first to Cat Spring and then branch out to other parts of the state.

Having left Houston, the newcomers soon realized that their life in Texas, unlike the idealistic picture portrayed in stories and letters, would not be easy. The rigors, uncertainties, and hardships exceeded anything for which life in Bohemia or Moravia had prepared them. J. Ustyník remembered that when he and his group made the journey in 1855, they did not have enough supplies because they had not expected such a deserted country. An early pioneer remembered how "those who had guns shot some birds and when we saw a farm we ran to ask if they had anything to eat but usually they did not have enough food for themselves."[15]

More disillusionment came in Cat Spring, the final destination for the first Czechs in Texas. In the early days of settlement (1850s), Cat Spring was nothing but a wooded prairie with "many wild cats. So we arrived at a spring, where our luggage was unloaded and where we were told: 'This is Cat Spring.'" The newcomers were bitterly disappointed; the women complained and some broke down and cried.[16]

Tomáš Krejča, from Moravia, recalled in his memoirs a Cat Spring businessman named Raimershofer, who had sent enticing letters to Moravia. The Raimershofers (or Reymershoffers) were one of the oldest families in Texas. Tomáš Čapek described the family as "passing through Cat Spring in 1855. Drifting to Galveston, they became prominent in business and politics there. John Reymershoffer, a son of the pioneer, acted as Austrian Consul."[17] But when Krejča and his group arrived in Cat Spring in 1855, they discovered that the idyllic portrait of Texas in Raimershofer's letters was not true. It turned out that Raimershofer, a store owner and land speculator, enticed the Czechs to Texas for purely self-serving reasons and wanted everybody to settle around Cat Spring (he was a counter-part to the Nebraska agent, Vodička, mentioned earlier).[18]

Patterns of settlement

Despite the disappointments, most early settlers decided to stay in Cat Spring. In time, Czechs spread out to the west and south (Fayette, Lavaca, and Washington Counties). Following the Civil War, they were attracted by the fertile soil of central Texas. One writer has described Cat Spring as the "mother settlement" for Texas Czechs. The oldest Czech settlement in Texas, Cat Spring was, for Czechs, the interior gateway to the Texas farm country. It spawned new Czech "daughter" settlements which gradually sprang up in several directions. The new communities remained attached to the "parent" Cat Spring community through family ties and friendships.[19]

Fayetteville, Industry, and Wesley were examples of daughter settlements. Petr Mikeška's story is apropos. Mikeška, a pioneer from Moravia, came to Cat Spring with his father via Houston in 1855. Petr lived with his father, who bought a farm and forty acres in Industry. Five years later, Petr married (a Czech). After renting a farm for two years, he bought forty-four acres near Wesley. Following the Civil War, Petr left Wesley for Lavaca County where he was able to buy 532 acres of land—in Bohemia only aristocrats and land barons had such large holdings.[20] If the story of František Branecký points up the hazards of emigration, Petr Mikeška's story helps to explain what attracted so many Czechs to the New World despite the risks and uncertainties—only in America could Czech peasants make the great leap from tenant to land baron!

In Texas, the Czechs generally settled near Germans. Those who went to school in the Old Country could speak German (the official language of the Austrian Empire of which the Czech lands were a part prior to World War I). The lifestyle and world view of the two ethnic groups were similar—both strove to be self-sufficient, dreamed of having a family farm, enjoyed dancing and beer drinking, and ate the same kind of food. The differences they had in Europe faded in the New World for practical as well as cultural reasons.

Czechs in the land of cotton

The first Texas Czechs depended on the Germans to help them make the transition to life in America. Germans came to Texas about two decades earlier and therefore were settled when the

Above: I. J. Gallia general store and post office, Engle, Texas, circa 1896. Photo courtesy of The Institute of Texan Cultures, San Antonio, Texas.

Below: J. R. Machu cash grocery store in Granger, Texas, circa 1903. Photo courtesy of The Institute of Texan Cultures, San Antonio, Texas.

Czechs arrived on the scene. They had learned some English and they knew how things worked. As Czech pioneers who knew some German probably spoke little or no English, they had to rely on Germans (who in some cases may even have spoken a little Czech) to show them the ropes.

The early pioneer years in the pre–Civil War period were hard for immigrant newcomers. As elsewhere, many Czechs in Texas could not afford to become farmers immediately, and so they had to find wage-earning jobs. But in Texas before the Civil War, the institution of slavery made it almost impossible to find such jobs. Many Czechs had no choice but to work in towns or to rent farm land.

Many Czech farmers at first mistakenly tilled the soil the way they were used to doing in Bohemia-Moravia. They had no experience growing either cotton or corn. They planted the seeds too close together. It was no wonder that yields were small. Skills such as carpentry were always useful since cash was badly needed to supplement the meager income from the crops in the first years.[21] Women often had to hoe the land while men went into cities to earn money.

In Texas, Czech farmers typically grew corn, cotton, tobacco, sugar cane, rye, yams, and fruit trees, and kept stock and poultry. The cotton and tobacco were grown for the market, the rest farmers grew to be self-sufficient.[22] As elsewhere, Czech farmers in Texas adopted a strategy of crop diversification to hedge against the risks of unpredictable and fluctuating prices for primary cash crops, especially cotton. They also avoided heavy borrowing. In time, this conservatism brought fruit, and most Texas Czechs prospered.[23]

The social structure of Czech migration from rural areas in Bohemia-Moravia was heterogeneous, but was dominated by the cottager class. Most settlers in Texas came from this class. Cottagers in the Old Country usually had a skill and owned land, but any chance of increasing their land holdings was nil or negligible. Land was a crucial factor in their lives because they depended on it for their livelihood—a feeling that the Czechs brought with them to the United States. The main goal remained to own land and pass it on to the next generation. In Czech communities it was considered a greater sin to neglect a farm than to get drunk on Saturday night or to skip church on Sunday morning.[24]

C.S.P.S. Lodge, a fraternal organization, in Granger, Texas. Photo courtesy of The Institute of Texan Cultures, San Antonio, Texas.

Kinship ties

The desire to acquire more land to pass along to one's children was strong. Old-timers advised Czech newcomers to move to smaller and younger communities because land was believed to be more expensive in the older settlements. The Czechs and Germans traditionally had large families and they bought most of the available land for their children. Thus, the best chance of getting a piece of land cheaply was near Americans, according to this view, because Americans traditionally had smaller families and children usually left the farm for city life. Thus, when the parents retired from farming the children sold the farm for a low price.[25] For whatever reason, many Czechs in Texas moved several times in search of cheaper and more fertile lands.[26]

The Czech newcomers followed a similar pattern everywhere they settled in Texas—they bought a farm, built a home, and later established churches, schools, and social or benevolent organizations.[27] Their social life and values set them apart from the rest of the ethnic groups in Texas. Tightly knit families and a strong bond to the land were the foundations on which Czech-American communities were built; Czech social and cultural life can be understood only in relation to this value system.[28]

The individual aspirations of a Czech farmer came second to the interests of his ethnic community. The closeness of the family unit transcended the family itself and carried over to the whole community. R. L. Skrabanek, in a study of Snook, a small predominantly Czech town northwest of Houston, found many forms of cooperation and mutual aid among the members of the community. In addition to being cohesive, Czech communities in Texas tended to be self-sufficient. There were stores and cooperatives, and Czechs shared labor as well as farm equipment. At harvest time, several families would work together and help each other bring in the crops. The women would cook together and several families would gather for feasts.[29] All neighborly help, whether in the fields or in times of need (for example, sickness or the death of a family member), would be reciprocal and no money would change hands.[30]

Skrabanek pointed out the "uniqueness of these practices in comparison to those of the non-Czechs who lived in the same county."[31] This was not a strategy so much as a way of life: it was the way Czechs had lived in the Old Country. In the New World it was natural to maintain the same social practices; but it was also a matter of survival because mutual assistance—a carry-over from the communal ways of Bohemian village life—was one of the keys to economic success for Czech-Americans.

In sum, the Czechs in Texas were industrious and ambitious; they bought into the American Dream, although they used the Old World methods to achieve it. Studies of Czechs in Texas suggest that Czech farmers readily adapted to the demands of a new environment, learning quickly how to grow cotton and tobacco despite the fact that they had never seen a cotton field or a tobacco patch before they came to Texas. But socio-culturally, Texas Czechs were resistant to change, retaining their language, customs, and traditions longer than most other immigrant groups.[32]

Chapter 9

 The Struggle for
Cultural Survival

Czechs settlers in the Midwest came from small villages in the Old
Country where the churches and taverns situated on the town
square were the center of social life, where relatives and neighbors
frequently gathered in each other's homes, and where a solitary life
was unimaginable. How did Czechs and Moravians cope with the
social deprivation associated with farming on the frontier, where
wide open spaces offered large plots of land but also separated them
from one another? And how did they organize for social and political
ends?

The economic challenges Czech immigrants faced were
matched by political, cultural, and social challenges no less formidable. They discovered that they could grow corn in the American
Midwest at least as well as they had grown wheat and flax in
Bohemia, but they were ill prepared to compete in a pluralistic
political order in which every group had to look out for its own
interests. The problem was not that they were incapable of compet-
ing in this arena, but rather that, in the absence of democratic
institutions, active participation in government was simply not part
of Czechs' political culture.

Religion: Roman Catholics vs. freethinkers

Czech Protestants from a community in Linn County, Iowa,
attended services at an English Protestant church on Sunday after-
noons, since on Sunday mornings the church belonged to the

English people. The language was a barrier. So was geography. For example, Josef Kostlán wrote in a letter to his parents in 1863 that it took him an hour to get to church. He also expressed disappointment over the lack of religious holidays in the United States.

Writing again in 1865, Kostlán observed that there were many Czechs, "both simple and educated," who did not care for God and eternity. When asked, "they say that religion is old-fashioned, some worship Nature, and others claimed to have left religion in the Old country." Kostlán's own opinion was that this freedom of religion was a good thing.[1] Nor was such a liberal attitude toward religion unusual. In fact, a majority of Czech immigrants "severed all formal ties with organized religion."[2] They became "freethinkers," believing that one could live a decent and honorable life without going to church.[3]

The freethinkers, who subscribed to an anti-clerical (primarily anti-Catholic), rational, and anti-Austrian movement, represent the only prominent political-philosophical tradition associated primarily with Czechs in America. With roots in the Czech lands dating back to the Revolution of 1848, the freethinking movement embraced "extension of civil liberties, absolute separation of church and state, introduction of universal suffrage, and gradual emancipation of women."[4] In the Czech lands, freethinking became a substitute for pan-Slavism, chronologically parallel to it but confined to the Czech part of the Austro-Hungarian Empire. In the United States, it was a respectable alternative to church-going, one which, among other things, relieved frugal Czech farmers of any obligation to tithe or otherwise financially support a church.

Most people who called themselves freethinkers were not atheists, but they eschewed organized religion. The freethinkers traced their origins to the Hussite reform movement of the fifteenth and sixteenth centuries—a movement, it should be noted, that was more nationalistic than religious.[5] They also had intellectual roots in the Enlightenment of the eighteenth century, as well as in German rationalism and socialism of the nineteenth century. Many Czechs rejected the Roman Catholic church because it was an ally of the Habsburg Empire, which for Czech nationalists became synonymous with political oppression following the ill-fated Protestant revolt of 1618, when Czechs were defeated by Austria at the Battle of White Mountain.[6]

Czechs were the only ethnic group in which freethinkers constituted an absolute majority. According to historian Bruce Garver:

> On the Great Plains and western prairies, the freethinking Czech language press helped to serve as the mind and conscience of Czech America and to maintain some sense of solidarity and common purpose among Czechs residing in widely scattered communities.[7]

In 1910, some 40 percent of all freethinkers lived in Nebraska, 32 percent lived in Texas, and the rest lived in other Great Plains states.[8]

The strength of freethinking varied with individuals, but suffered from the same crusading zeal on one extreme that characterized conventional religions, a condition which eventually alienated the younger generation.[9] By the 1920s, the movement was on the wane.

Given the freedom to choose any religion, many Czechs thus chose none. It is tempting to attribute the Czech propensity for freethinking to anti-Catholicism, but the truth is that, "They were free to adopt some form of Protestantism if they preferred it to Catholicism, but they did not."[10]

Czech Protestants were a small minority, numbering about 5 percent.[11] A group of Protestants, known as the Evangelicals of the Reformed Church, settled near Cedar Rapids, Iowa, in the early 1860s. Too poor to build a church, they held Sunday services in private homes. Occasionally they went to Ely, nine miles from Cedar Rapids, to hear sermons by Reverend Francis Kůň. Josef Kostlán wrote in a letter, "We have here some preacher from Moravia, his name is Kůň. He is a wise man and a good orator." The church in Ely, organized in 1858, was the first Czech Protestant church in the United States.[12] (It was not until 1880 that the Czech Reformed Church was formally organized in Cedar Rapids.)

Despite their liberal views on organized religion, Czechs continued to celebrate holidays on the Catholic calendar. These holidays were an important part of peasant traditions in Bohemia and Moravia, so the celebrations represented a link to the Czech homeland.[13] Thus, some of the pagan rituals taken over by the church in Europe continued to play a role in the lives of Czech settlers in America.

The Roman Catholic Church in America tried to keep Czechs within the fold, but with limited success. An estimated 40 percent of the Czechs who remained loyal to the Roman Catholic Church rejected clericalism (the hierarchical authority of the priesthood in secular as well as spiritual matters) and believed the church should be stripped of the political power it exercised in the Austro-Hungarian Empire.[14]

The dominant role of the Irish in Catholic churches may have been a cause of low church attendance in Czech communities. Many Czechs could not understand English very well and therefore may not have felt comfortable attending the masses (even though mass was said in Latin until recently). Memoirs of the Czech pioneers indicate that in the Old Country they were not accustomed to giving money to church. Many Czech settlers apparently left organized religion in the United States because they did not want (or could not afford) to make contributions.[15]

The decline of church attendance was symptomatic of a change in moral values and attitudes among Czechs, according to an editor of the freethinking Czech weekly *Pokrok Západu*, when he wrote in 1877 that "there are German and Irish Catholic priests in Omaha and they cannot do much for Czechs there (in rural areas)," and as a result,

> many live without religion, children are not christened either because families live too far from the church, or they cannot make arrangements with a priest. Couples live together without getting married because they are under an influence of sects that have their agents everywhere.[16]

In response, the archdiocese in St. Louis sponsored immigration of individual Catholic priests from Bohemia to Nebraska. The aim, of course, was to revitalize the church in areas where Czechs were settling by giving services in the Czech language. This program was hampered by the prevalence and power of freethinking among Nebraska Czechs during the early settlement period.

Some individuals yearned for spiritual guidance. A farmer in Brown County lamented the absence of a Catholic church in the vicinity. He had hoped that more Czech Catholics would settle in the county, making the chances of building a church greater. With a heavy heart, he recalled the previous Christmas on the prairie when he had read out of his prayer book to his family and sang psalms together with his wife and a small daughter. The experience helped him to feel as if he were at home for a while.

> I remembered you, my dear fellow countrymen, living in cities, how you feel during these special Christmas days, while I, farmer, celebrate Christmas in solitude and sadness in this spiritual desert here. We have plenty of meat, bread, eggs and coffee but spiritual goods we have none.[17]

The relative strength of Catholic Moravians in Saunders and Butler Counties led to the founding of the first Czech Catholic church in Nebraska in 1876, in the town of Abie (Butler County).[18] A few years later, in 1879, a Czech priest, having arrived from Bohemia, visited numerous Czech farms in Saline County, southwest of Lincoln, in an effort to raise money for a Catholic church in Wilber. But he ran into a stone wall of freethinking—among the farmers in Saline County freethinkers outnumbered Catholics.[19] The upshot: no contributions, no church.

The dividing line in Czech social life was usually religion. Take, for example, Josef Blažek of Smetana, Texas. Blažek cited religious reasons for emigrating from Moravia. He was disgusted with what he saw as the hypocrisy of Catholic church officials. In Texas, he became a "freethinker" and participated in something called the "Plow and Book." On learning that many members were conservative Catholics he promptly left the group.[20]

Leaders of the Protestant churches were frequently vocal in expressing their antagonism towards the freethinkers. Czech Brethren from Cedar Rapids, Iowa, charged that the agnostic and often atheistic ideas of the freethinkers took away the hope and faith in a "higher form of life," and led to high suicide rates among Czech settlers.[21] There is evidence that the suicide rate for Czech-American farmers *was* higher than average. Czech Protestants, rightly or wrongly, blamed freethinking for this disturbing phenomenon.

Of course, not all Czechs were as adamant about religious matters as Josef Blažek in Texas or the Czech Brethren in Iowa. Clinton Machan notes that in Texas, for example, there were interdominational marriages, and cites cases of Protestant Czech schools catering to children from Catholic families.[22]

Politics, populism, and prohibition

Political activity in the Czech lands had been greatly circum-
scribed by the emperor prior to 1867, when the government passed
a law that allowed freedom of assembly. Notwithstanding this
change, Czech immigrants to the United States had little or no direct
experience in political affairs—a fact which may help to explain why
Czechs in Nebraska, unlike Scandinavians in Minnesota, seldom
got involved in politics or held high office. There were, of course,
rare exceptions, such as Tomáš Čapek of Omaha, who became the
first Czech immigrant to win election as a Democrat to the Nebraska
House of Representatives in 1890.

Many immigrants had vague and loosely defined ideas about
political freedom in the United States. Yearning for political freedom was only one reason among many why Czechs came to the
United States. Indeed, politics appears to have played a relatively
minor role in Czech migration in the nineteenth century, with one
exception—the period immediately following the Revolution of
1848.

The most significant political immigration came in the middle
of the nineteenth century. Political immigrants often had great
expectations and overestimated the amount of freedom they would
enjoy in America. In general, European radical ideals of 1848 did not
blossom in the New World. Most immigrants from the post-1848 era
were left-wing intellectuals, impatient with the middle-class liberal
ideals that dominated the political atmosphere of nineteenth-century American politics. Many of these immigrants (early freethinkers), such as Vojtěch Náprstek, became disillusioned and returned
to the Czech lands when it was safe; some died forgotten in the
United States.

Nebraska Czechs stood apart from the radical element in
Czech-American politics. They came from humble origins in rural
areas in the Czech lands where political life was, at best, in a
rudimentary stage. As noted earlier, Czech farmers had not left their
homeland for political reasons. The political concerns that influenced their thinking were mirrored in the ideas of the urban-based
Czech National Revival Movement of the eighteenth and early
nineteenth centuries, which stressed the value of folk culture and of
the Czech language. The ideas of the National Revival Movement
were ultimately doomed to failure in the New World because the

forces of assimilation and the imperative to learn English were too powerful to combat or resist in the long run.

Newspaper articles and letters reflected the level of political consciousness of the Czech settlers. Czechs in Nebraska published two daily newspapers, *Pokrok Západu*, published in Omaha since 1871, and *Nová Doba* (*New Era*) in Schuyler, Colfax County. Czechs were primarily concerned with one "lifestyle" issue: "Prohibition and other symbols of the clash between native and immigrant cultures" were the main items appearing in *Pokrok Západu*.[23] Having come from a country were the government restricted such "abstract" liberties as freedom of speech and assembly, Czech immigrants found that American society was, in one key area of great importance to their way of life, far more restrictive. What had been a natural element in social interactions of all kinds, an integral part of all happy occasions in the Old Country—i.e., consumption of alcohol—was stigmatized as the work of the devil by Bible-thumping "tee-totallers" in the United States.

Most Czechs voted ethnically rather than ideologically. A majority of Czech-Moravians supported the Democratic party, which they perceived as an anti-prohibition party. Basically, Czechs wanted to be free to think and do as they pleased, and the only real threat to their way of life in rural America was the anti-immigration, nativist, and prohibitionist Women's Christian Temperance Union (WCTU), which dated from 1874, and the Anti-Saloon League after 1893. Both groups were associated with the Republican party, which goes far toward explaining why most Czechs in America were Democrats. After 1869, there was actually a Prohibition party in the United States; this party ran candidates for public office beginning in 1876. The Anti-Saloon League forced the prohibition issue into the forefront of state and local elections across the nation in the 1890s.[24] It is noteworthy that the emergence of a powerful reformist movement—fueled above all by opposition to alcohol consumption in the United States (similar in some ways to the anti-drug movement today)—coincides with the most intense period of Czech immigration, 1870–1900.

The anti-"dry" faction within the Czech community became increasingly vocal, particularly after the restrictions on the sale of alcohol came into effect in 1881. Only a few could afford to purchase the license to sell alcohol prior to 1880; the fee was five hundred dollars—an enormous restriction.[25] Among other issues raised by the new alcohol regime was the sale of alcohol on Sundays; not surprisingly, many Czechs were anti-Sabbatarians.

While most Czechs (like the majority of Germans) were vehemently "wet," a few Czech temperance supporters originated in predominantly Catholic Butler County, Nebraska. Advocating moderation in drinking and tobacco chewing, they represented a conservative element within the Czech community. "We tend to accept the bad habits of this country," wrote one disgruntled reader in *Pokrok Západu* in 1881. "Too much alcohol is bad for one's health and sets a bad example for the children."[26]

Aside from prohibition, which was a national issue, Czechs were generally uninterested in high politics.[27] In a letter found in the Náprstek collection in Prague, for example, the author lamented the fact that Czech-Americans had "not grown to appreciate the cultural significance of American freedom . . . [and] do not understand its origins, cause and its structure."[28] At elections, the Czech voter was unsophisticated and "inclined to vote for one of his nationality, regardless of his political convictions or connections."[29] To some extent, any tendency to avoid politics may have been rooted in habits formed over centuries of external political domination in the Czech lands. For Bohemian and Moravian peasants, politics was something very remote from village life. The seat of imperial rule was not Prague, itself distant and inaccessible, but Vienna—a world apart. The language of politics and government was German, not Czech.

Thus, Czech immigrant-farmers in Nebraska, many of whom had been small landholders and hired laborers living in rural villages in southern Bohemia and southwestern Moravia only a few years earlier, had little or no sense of political efficacy or potential. Politically, Czech peasants did not count in Austria-Hungary. In the United States, things did not seem so different. The national capital, Washington, D.C., was distant. The language of politics, English, was alien. And Czech immigrants formed an inarticulate minority— in other words, they did not count. It was an all-too-familiar situation, but with a cruel twist. In the Czech lands, they formed a majority and they did not have to defend their folkways. In America, with the tempest of prohibition raging, they did. To the extent that Czech-Americans later became involved in politics, it was an orientation they had to acquire after they came to America.

The political issues that concerned them, combined with their relatively low level of active participation in political organizations, testified to the narrow world-view of Czech and Moravian immigrants whose "Czech consciousness" or coherence and cohesion as a political force never went beyond the short-lived National Revival stage. Although Czechs claimed to support universal liberty, they opposed women's right to vote—a contradiction which reflected the patriarchal tradition of Czech society and, more important, their alarm at the temperance movement being spearheaded by women activists in the 1870s and 1880s.

In keeping with their political inertia, Czechs showed little interest in American farmers organizations despite the popularity of cooperatives in rural communities in the Czech lands. The Grangers' movement and the Farmers' Alliances with their "goals of cooperative marketing, buying and production gained relatively few consistent adherents" among farmers before 1900.[30] Lack of Czech support was also due to the Farmers' Alliance connection to the populists, a political movement that was anathema to Czech ideas and cultural heritage—the populists were strongly Anglo-Saxon nativist and prohibitionist.[31]

A word about the link between nativism and populism on the prairie is in order. A resurgence of nativism occurred in the 1880s and was "devoted to saving the country from imaginary papal conspiracies." The most successful of these nativist groups, known as the American Protective Association (APA), operated mainly in the Protestant strongholds of the upper Mississippi valley. Between 1887 and 1893, the APA reached its zenith, aided by popular fears and frustrations resulting from the economic depression of the early 1890s. After 1893, the APA gave way to populists and free-silver advocates, who took up the APA's pet causes, including "restricted immigration, more stringent naturalization requirements, refusal to employ aliens or Catholics, and the teaching of the 'American' language in schools."[32]

Thus, the tendency of Czechs to stay away from high politics can be seen as rational. A relatively small group of newcomers, greatly outnumbered by Anglo-Saxon "Americans," many Czechs may have reasoned that the best approach was to assume a low profile and hope that the wrath of the majority would not come down on them. Except, of course, for prohibition: the one threat that was apparently too important not to meet head-on because drinking was so integral to Czech social life and culture.

If this hypothesis has any merit, it follows that focusing on a single issue, the one that was clearly most important to the great majority of Czechs, whatever their religious or political leanings, made sense. As a recently arrived minority group, Czechs had limited political power under the best of circumstances (a condition to which they were accustomed as members of a subjugated nation within the Austro-Hungarian Empire) and were divided along ethnic (Czech vs. Moravian), religious (Catholic vs. Freethinker), and geographic lines (Czechs and Moravians tended to settle in adjacent areas but not in the same locales) in the Midwest. As we shall see, Czechs were also divided along socio-economic lines on certain issues. The one thing they could nearly all agree on was that prohibition had to be stopped.

One other issue of immediate importance to Czech immigrants in the Midwest was the power of the railroads. In the 1880s the Farmers' Alliance, which sought railroad regulation, currency inflation, anti-trust laws, and affordable farm credit, had the support of many beginning farmers.[33] Czechs from Butler County, Nebraska, actually founded a Czech branch of the Farmers' Alliance in 1882; there was also some support from Czechs in Saunders County, Nebraska.[34] But many relatively wealthy Czech farmers lost interest in common action against the monopoly of railroads—they could, after all, afford to pay the high tariffs. Hence, the railroad issue ultimately revealed the existence of class differences among Czechs. The established farmers could literally afford to "pay the freight" to have their crops shipped to market, while the neophyte farmers could not.

Fraternal organizations

Organizations exclusively for Czechs were popular among the first generation of Czech immigrants, a fact which could also explain the small numbers of Czechs joining the American farmers' organizations and movements. The language barrier was a major consideration in understanding the political behavior of first-generation Czech immigrants.

Czechs' strong support of fraternal organizations, the backbone of freethinking in rural America, was an outer expression of a

Bohemian band in Nebraska circa 1896. Photo courtesy of Nebraska State Historical Society.

deep-seated insecurity, a feeling common to all farmers.[35] These organizations had two principal functions: to serve as social support systems and to provide insurance for their members.

Czechs saw insurance against natural disasters as the solution to one of the farmers' many problems, an idea which originated in the Old Country. Czech fraternal organizations in the United States provided protection against physical injury and often included life insurance, as well. For example, the national Česko-Slovanský Podpůrný Spolek (Č.S.P.S.), a fraternal insurance organization founded in 1854, had branches in most Czech settlements and survives to this date. Another organization called Český rolnický vespolný výpomocný spolek (Czech Peasant Mutual Help Association) was founded in 1876. Its purpose was to insure members against hail damage to wheat, rye, barley, oats, flax, and corn. In 1897, the westerners quit the Č.S.P.S. and formed the Západní Česká Bratrská Jednota (Western Fraternal Life Association). At the same time, Tex-Czechs formed the Slovanská podporující jednota státu Texasu (Slavonic Benevolent Order of the State of Texas).[36]

The fraternal orders maintained lodges in the Czech communities where they had a presence. The lodges had social functions. On special occasions, wives were permitted to accompany their husbands.[37] In Box Butte County, Nebraska, for example, a lodge still stands near the spot where a Bohemian Catholic church was recently demolished. As late as 1989, according to two Czech old-timers, the building was used for a dance. In the early days, such lodges were alternatives to churches where Czechs (especially Freethinkers) could meet, drink and dance, and talk Czech. The two elderly Czech farmers in Box Butte expressed nostalgia for the good old days when the lodge was a lively center of social activity.[38]

Areas with heavy concentrations of Czechs usually supported the Sokol gymnastic organization. Sokol (Falcon) founded in 1862 in Bohemia, was a fraternal organization with nationalistic undertones. Membership in Sokol had no financial benefits; the aim of the organization was physical prowess. Czechs donated money and work to build Sokol halls. Library groups attached to Sokol halls perpetuated the language and educated the public.

Czech reading and dramatic societies were popular in Iowa, Minnesota, and elsewhere in the Midwest, particularly among the freethinkers. The creation of these societies and clubs was an expression of Czech devotion to their culture, language, and customs. A specific example is Slovanská lípa (Slav Linden), a cultural patriotic organization with chapters in many Midwestern Czech-American communities in the nineteenth century. The various local chapters of Slovanská lípa established libraries and supported programs of Czech music, drama, and dancing.

In Iowa, the Reading Society (Čtenářský spolek) was established already in 1868 in Cedar Rapids.[39] Both women and men participated in the programs and in time the organization had chapters in most Czech communities in Iowa. The members promoted teaching of the Czech language, putting on plays, and readings of Czech works. They also celebrated anniversaries of Jan Hus (a fifteenth-century Catholic church reformer), Jan Ámos Komenský (a seventeenth-century Czech educational reformer), and of important historical events.[40] Farmers attended most of these festivals. In 1870, for example, farmers and their families arriving in fourteen wagons were met by the band and by a group of Czech girls when they came to celebrate Jan Hus Day in Cedar Rapids.[41]

Education

"Tell teacher Jarošovský that there is no prospect for him here. There is no plan to start Czech schools. So, if he wants to come, he should plan on a different career." Thus did Josef Kostlán comment on the state of education in rural Iowa in the 1860s. Education was always important to Czechs, but on the American frontier schools were a luxury the early settlers could not afford.

Generally, Czechs supported public school education and thus contributed to the assimilation process.[42] Education was important to Czech immigrants. "We shall leave them property which they may lose but education is an investment which will only generate an interest."[43]

During the harvest, farmers needed their children's help and the time had to be divided between the school and the farm. In Texas, for example, the children left school as soon as they were old enough to work as farm hands. Only a few children continued with their education beyond grammar school.[44]

A disappearing heritage

Early Czech settlers enjoyed a rich social life that broke up the monotony of farm work. Dancing and picnics were common in Czech settlements. The dances were frequent—one or more a week, and Czechs happily contributed both money and labor to the building of the dance halls.[45] These traditional patterns of social and cultural interaction, however, gradually died out.

By the 1880s, the assimilation process had taken its toll. Only a few Czech communities in Nebraska, for example, made a last effort at a revival of the Czech language. The Czech-American children learned Czech in Sunday schools, while children of other nationalities had religious education.[46] In 1891, Czechs in Schuyler (Colfax County), for instance, lost a Czech school due to the lack of community interest.[47]

The second generation growing up in the United States felt far removed from traditional Czech culture, which young Czechs regarded as old-fashioned—a prime example of the generation gap a century before the concept was popularized. The plays written in the National Revival style in the Czech lands or in the United States, for instance, meant very little to the children born in the United States.

Towards the end of the century, at a time when important anniversaries from Czech history were no longer celebrated by the settlers, a few Czech people began to voice criticism and skepticism of the Czech-American cultural and national life. In 1873 Czechs in Wilber, Nebraska, for the first time ever commemorated the death of Jan Hus, the famous Czech martyr who was burned at the stake on July 6, 1415.[48] In 1887, Czechs in nearby Crete observed this traditional Czech holiday, but its historical significance was only a side issue to a dancing celebration. In the 1890s, many Czechs began to feel that they were without value to the Czech nation:

> We rejected our motherland because of greed, not for the ideal of freedom but in search of the whiter bread. Our patriotism has no purpose, it is just a shallow attempt to feed senseless conceit. We create our little celebrations and play anthems but they are only a facade painted with a false patriotism. What have we achieved? Czech schools are left in neglect, the sole purpose of our fraternal organizations are perennial dances and picnics. Our language will die with us and our children will never learn anything from us.[49]

Epilogue

A Czech visitor at the turn of the century noted that Czechs in America were left with "a love for the Czech language and that was all." Most Czech immigrants to the United States had little or no first-hand knowledge of Prague, the center of Czech cultural life. On the contrary, they were familiar with life in their native village, and little else. Culture, for these rural Czechs, was folk culture, not high culture.[50] Hence, it is not surprising that what survived longest were Czech folkways and language, while the most distinctive national achievements of Czechs in literature, art, music, and the like, were largely ignored—a situation that most other ethnic groups experienced also.

Czechs missed some aspects of the life in a Czech village, but the material benefits of farming in the Midwest outweighed any sense of loss.[51] Feelings of loneliness, however, were common. Nebraska, Iowa, and parts of Texas appeared deserted and lifeless to the casual observer, in stark contrast to the Czech countryside which was dotted with villages and ever-present signs of human activity. In Bohemia and Moravia, hills and woods created a feeling of warmth and security singularly absent on the wide-open and windswept Great Plains. In the rather featureless Nebraska landscape, for example, farm buildings scattered around a dusty countryside with bad roads connecting the settlements lacked the picturesque atmosphere of a Czech or Moravian village. The first pioneers' houses were either sod houses or primitive wooden structures described by J. Štolba in 1891 as "huts suitable for cows in Bohemia."[52]

Notwithstanding, the letters from Czech-American farmers printed in Czech newspapers do not reflect misgivings; instead, they overwhelmingly indicate a satisfaction with the decision to emigrate. A farmer from Colfax County, Nebraska, wrote how in 1875 he decided to leave his "motherland and sold everything for one thousand guldens." He continued:

> I set off on a journey with my family. I received homestead, I bought two bulls for one hundred and thirty six dollars, one cow for thirty-two dollars and a stove for the same price and all my money was gone. Different setbacks started but I succeeded in all. Now I live well, I have three hundred and twenty acres, five horses and thirty-five herd of cattle. I bought a house for seven hundred dollars and in 1885 barns for three hundred dollars. I think that the United States is good for a poor person because here a person sees that hard work brings results.[53]

Getting started was difficult and Czechs often experienced feelings of insecurity. As an ethnic group they settled close to each other in order to create a support network and perpetuate the folkways of the Old Country. They hung on to their language and used it by putting on plays. They organized dances and picnics. They also belonged to fraternal lodges that gave them material security and a sense of community, which was important to them. The Czech language separated them from other ethnic groups. Among the major farming groups, Czech was the only Slavic and non-Germanic language, which made any communication with the rest of the settlers more complicated. Many Czechs could communicate with Germans, but preferred to live near other Czechs.

Their religion or the lack of it also set them apart. They did not go to the churches because they did not understand the sermon or they simply rejected the former spiritual life. Thus the number of contacts the first generation of Czechs had with the other groups in the Midwest was minimal, and therefore their acculturation was slow.

As agricultural producers, Czechs were quite successful, adapting to the extent necessary to cope with new conditions. In social, religious, and cultural realms, however, the acculturation process was slower. Circumstances did not force Czechs to change in their life, except in the economic realm. In farming, old methods gave way to an efficient and profitable mode of production, while in the spiritual life in its broadest sense "Czech" characteristics were retained much longer.

Unidentified Nebraska farmstead. Photo courtesy of Nebraska State Historical Society.

Chapter 10

 Summary and
Conclusions

Czech immigrants to the United States had to adjust to a new environment, but for those who came to the Midwest the ultimate challenge was to make the transition from village peasant to frontier farmer. This transformation was a complex process which Czech-Moravian immigrants managed successfully, as measured by such standards as economic position and social mobility. The Czechs in America illustrate the limited validity of Frederick Jackson Turner's concept of the frontier as a crucible in which "old world" characteristics are melted down because it was precisely these characteristics that allowed transplanted Czech peasants to cope with the harsh conditions in the Midwest and in Texas.

The nineteenth-century mass emigration from the Czech lands dates from the 1860s and reached its peak in the 1880s. This phenomenon was one of the by-products of the Industrial Revolution in the Austro-Hungarian Empire, where the patchwork of industrialization left large areas untouched by the modern age. Thus, the course of European social, economic, and political history is connected by invisible threads stretching from Bohemia and Moravia across the Atlantic to improbable places such as Texas, Iowa, and Nebraska.

Although this study stresses the economic and social causes of Czech-Moravian emigration, it was a political change in the Austro-Hungarian Empire that opened the flood gates. A series of liberal laws passed in 1867 created a new political system based on the principle of constitutional monarchy. These measures made all citizens equal in the eyes of the law (although it was not until 1907 that the franchise was extended to all adult citizens) and established such civil liberties as freedom of movement (the right to emigrate), freedom of expression, and freedom of assembly (which led to formation of political clubs, precursors of political parties).

The new laws also had economic implications, not least of which was the fact that peasants gained the right for the first time to dispose of their property at will. This change exacerbated an already nettlesome situation—children inherited tiny fragments of land insufficient for a livelihood. The number of landless peasants increased as the richest landowners amassed more and more land. These land barons dictated grain market prices, controlled the rudimentary banking and credit system, and drove small operators out of business.

As emigration applications show, many immigrants left because the future was bleak for smallholders—ironically, the same reason why many small farmers in the Midwest today are "getting out." Czech peasants also feared a loss of social status. Reassuring letters from relatives and friends in the United States promised a better life and made the decision to leave home easier. In some cases, immigrants even received ship tickets in the mail from loved ones who had "made it" in America.

The migration process started in the late 1860s, gained momentum in the 1870s and 1880s, peaked in the late 1880s, gradually slowed until 1900, surged again after 1900, until it was brought to an abrupt halt by the onset of the First World War in 1914.

The emigration epidemic hit hardest in a belt stretching from southwestern Bohemia to southwestern Moravia. The earliest immigrants—many of whom went to Texas—came from northeastern Bohemia and northern Moravia. The oldest emigration area was in western Bohemia, while the foothills of the Czech-Moravian Highlands was the last area to be affected.

Czech immigrants did not start arriving in America in large numbers until the 1870s. By that time, most of the good land east of the Mississippi was already taken. Having settled first in cities such as New York, Cleveland, Chicago, and St. Louis, many were drawn westward by the allure of free land and the frontier. Some were no doubt nostalgic for the agrarian life they had left behind in Bohemia or Moravia. Others may have been looking for adventure.

For Czechs living in Chicago, Wisconsin was just around the bend. Some who went to Wisconsin stayed; many discovered that most of the good land was already taken and that the price of land was beyond their means. So they went further west, to Minnesota, Iowa, Nebraska, Kansas, and the Dakotas. In so doing, they started a movement. Other Czechs followed, and by the 1880s what started as a trickle had become a steady stream.

Czechs had left Bohemia and Moravia because they believed America was the land of opportunity. The greatest opportunities in the last quarter of the nineteenth century were in the West. It so happened that America's breadbasket—a vast region stretching from the Mississippi to the Rocky Mountains—was opening up at precisely the time when Czechs were arriving in the greatest numbers. It was also the case that most Czech immigrants came from rural areas in Bohemia and Moravia and, whether or not they had been tillers of the soil in the old country, they were very much at home in a rural setting. This was especially true of those who settled in Nebraska.

The census data and a contemporary survey of the Czech population tell a story about the significance of Czech settlers in Nebraska. They formed 6–9 percent of all the foreign-born population over the four decades of the nineteenth century, and 2 percent of the total Nebraska population. Czechs and Moravians came from a highly diffuse area and there was little regularity in their settlement patterns with respect to Czech and Moravian villages. They came because their relatives or friends had settled in the state, they read about Nebraska through advertisements in newspapers and pamphlets, from agents of immigration companies and railroads. Moravians, more than the Czechs, had friends and/or relatives in Nebraska whom they followed directly from the port.

Most Czech immigrants to rural America came from the cottager class. This class was by no means the poorest but those who belonged to it often "felt the pinch of adversity" in the nineteenth century. Despite the fact that they were landowners in the Old Country, they had little hope of self-improvement due to recurrent economic depressions in rural areas, population pressure on land resources, and changes in land tenure laws. By contrast, rural

America was a land of opportunity. A place to farm, to raise a family, and to build a future.

On the frontier, Czechs and Moravians adopted a strategy of risk-limitation by growing a variety of crops, an approach that required a large initial investment but protected the farmers against a sharp drop in the price of a particular crop. The two characteristics brought with them—an aversion to borrowing money and a propensity to limit risks—are linked and largely account for their economic success as frontier farmers. The Czech immigrants' near-obsession with financial security, a trait born of the gnawing insecurity that had driven them from the Old Country, is no doubt one reason why they had significantly higher success rates than other ethnic groups settled in the same areas. Observed over a period of ten years, most Czech-American farmers stayed put, did not incur debts or financial losses, and generally prospered.

Although there were some specific differences between the Czechs who came to Texas and those who settled in the Midwest, Texas Czechs were like Czech-American farmers everywhere in certain essential ways. First, they all made a virtue out of necessity. Second, strong familial ties and a love of the land helped them to meet the challenges of pioneering in a strange land. Third, a conservative strategy of crop diversification and mutual assistance are two keys to the economic success of Czechs in Texas.

Their cultural life never went beyond a Czech National Revival Movement (stressing the importance of the language and folk traditions). This low cultural level betrayed their rural origins and lack of education. Czech immigrants came from economically depressed rural areas and so it is hardly surprising that they were intellectually and culturally unsophisticated. They emigrated primarily for economic reasons, not to escape political oppression or to seek personal freedom.

Voting patterns suggest that Czechs and Moravians were a cohesive ethnic group, but they lacked direct experience in representative government. As a consequence, they were slow to take advantage of the political liberties and opportunities for participation in self-rule the United States offered.

Czech immigrants often disguised this socio-economic motivation under the cloak of disaffection with Habsburg tyranny. Talk of a desire to escape autocratic rule always plays well in America, as any immigrant knows. The forefathers of Midwestern and Texas Czechs, however, did not flee religious or political oppression. They were not refugees or asylum-seekers. Nor were they visionary radicals. They were simple peasants in search of land. They found it in "America."

Appendix A
Researching Czech Ancestry

Czech-Americans interested in tracing their roots back to the Old Country should begin with the Czechoslovak Genealogical Society in St. Paul, Minnesota, or the Cultural Council at the Czech Embassy in Washington, D.C. For a fee, the council will contact the National Archive in Czechoslovakia. It is wise to do a little research into your family background before you contact the embassy. As much available data as possible should be sent with the initial inquiry.

If readers prefer to go to The Czech Republic and do the research themselves, that is also quite possible. It is a good excuse to visit The Czech Republic and it is a "mission" that can turn a sight-seeing trip into a real adventure. The excitement of finding out first-hand about one's family history and walking in the footsteps of one's ancestors is difficult to exaggerate.

All the available records older than fifty years are accessible to the public. The archival records are kept in the State Central Archive (SÚa) in Prague, in the regional archives (Státní Oblastní archív), and in district archives (Okresní archív).

If the Czech region of emigration is not known

Czech-Americans who do not know the specific region in The Czech Republic from which their ancestors left should begin by contacting the regional archives because they have the lists of all emigrants. Copies of these emigration lists are also kept in the State Central Archive (SÚa) in Prague.

Unfortunately, genealogical research never comes with an ironclad guarantee of success. In the case of Czech emigrants, the lists are incomplete, since they do not include all the legal emigrants, and no record could have been made of the illegal emigrants. Also, these lists do not cover the entire period between 1848–1914. And people travelling with a passport as "tourists" who decided not to return do not appear on the lists at all.

Nonetheless, persistence usually pays off. For individuals who do not know their family's specific region of origin, the best place to start is the Czechoslovak Genealogical Society in St. Paul,

Minnesota. An advertisement in *Naše rodina* (*Our Family*), a publication of this society, is one possible way to find somebody in the United States who has further information. This magazine is in circulation in approximately forty states of the Union.

If the Czech region of emigration is known

If the region of emigration is known, the initial inquiry should be sent directly to the state regional archive of the appropriate region. Alternatively, the researcher may travel to the corresponding regional archive, having first found it on the map or asked the Czech Embassy to which region the village belongs. The state regional archives are in Prague (central Czech region), in Třeboň (southern), in Plzeň (western), in Litoměřice (northern), in Zámrsk (eastern), in Brno (south Moravian), and in Opava (north Moravian).

Information about the dates of birth, marriage, and death in the Czech lands of at least one ancestor or of the emigrant about whom the inquiry is being made should be included in the inquiry. The state regional archives keep these in their holdings. Prior to 1950, such records were kept in parishes. After 1950, they were moved to district archives. During the 1960s, the records were moved again to the present sites—to the regional archives. The records are by villages.

Information about the religion of the ancestor(s) is also important, since the records of birth were filed according to the faith of the parents. Specific information about the ancestor's place of residence or birth is especially important. The fact that somebody came from, say, the Čáslav region is not specific enough, since this region included forty villages at one time. The rule of thumb in genealogical research is a simple one: the more accurate the information you start with—the road map, so to speak—the more quickly you will get to your destination.

Even if you know the name of your ancestor's village, you may be in for a surprise. It is possible that there are five villages with the same name located in five different regions! Thus, it is beneficial to find out the region (*oblast/kraj*) or the district (*okres*) of the village. Supplying a passport or a work book with the inquiry helps the researcher who is then able to look for an official rubber stamp or other details that otherwise might go unnoticed by someone not accustomed to doing genealogical research.

As noted earlier, the records of birth, marriage, and death are kept in the regional state archives, and not in the villages the emigrants left. Some towns and villages—those with a local government (*obecní úřad*)—began to keep vital statistics at the beginning of the twentieth century.

A regional archive often keeps the lists of records of its district archival possessions. Under umbrella of the regional archive in Prague are district archives in Prague-west, Prague-east, Mělník, Nymburk, Mladá Boleslav, Kolín, Kutná Hora, Benešov, Příbram, Beroun, Rakovník, and Kladno. Under the regional archive in Třeboň are Pelhřimov, Jindřichův Hradec, Tábor, České Budějovice, Český Krumlov, Prachatice, Písek, and Strakonice. The district archives of Klatovy, Domažlice, Plzeň-south, City of Plzeň, Plzeň-north, Rokycany, Tachov, Cheb, and Karlovy Vary are in the Plzeň region.

In addition to Prague, Třeboň, and Plzeň, there are four other regional centers with lists of records from archival districts. The Litoměrice region includes Chomutov, Most, Louny, Teplice, Děčín, Ústí nad Labem, Česká Lípa, Litoměrice, Liberec, and Jablonec nad Nisou. The regional archive in Zámrsk has the following district archives under its jurisdiction: Semily, Jičín, Trutnov, Náchod, Hradec Králové, Rychnov nad Kněžnou, Pardubice, Chrudim, Ústí nad Orlicí, and Havlíčkův Brod. In the regional archive of southern Moravia located at Brno are the district archives of Břeclav, Znojmo, Třebíč, Jihlava, Žďár nad Sázavou, Blansko, Prostějov, Vyškov, Kroměříž, Zlín, Uherské Hradište, Hodonín, Brno-rural districts, and the city of Brno. Finally, northern Moravia includes the districts of Šumperk, Bruntál, Olomouc, Přerov, Nový Jičín, Vsetín, Frýdek-Místek, Karviná, and Ostrava under the regional archive in Opava.

As a rule, materials relevant to a particular region (passport information, land property, ownership of real estate) are kept in district (*okresní*) archives. If a village belonged to a large manor which had its own archive, information pertaining to the ancestral real estate could be found in the regional archive for that village.

Nebraska-Kansas immigrants, 1891–1895

Researchers whose ancestors immigrated to Nebraska and parts of Kansas in 1891–1895 should consult *Nebraska, Kansas Czech Settlers, 1891–1895*, compiled by Margie Sobotka of Omaha, Nebraska. Based on a nineteenth-century survey by Frank Mareš,

Sobotka compiled lists of names and data including employment, and village and region of origin of Czech settlers in Nebraska and Kansas.

For further information about genealogical research in Czechoslovakia, the reader should contact The Czechoslovak Genealogical Society, P.O. Box 16225, St. Paul, Minnesota 55516. The society offers many resources. They can also refer you to individuals who do private research. Readers with questions about archival research in Czechoslovakia, as well as anyone who has (or knows about) materials bearing on the history on Czech-American immigration, are also encouraged to contact Štěpánka Korytová-Magstadt by writing to the publisher of this book.

Maps

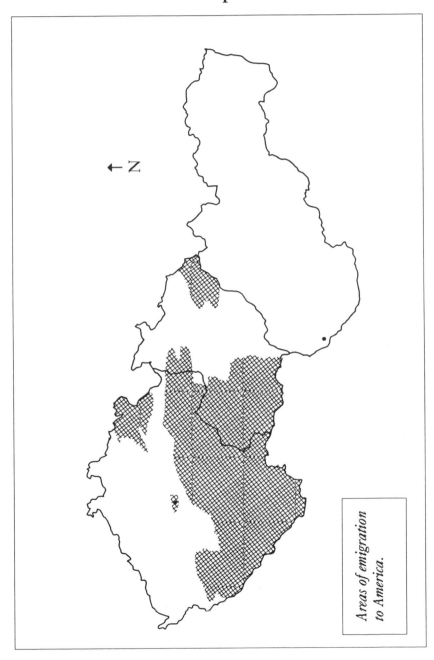

N ←

*Areas of emigration
to America.*

Primary areas of emigration to the Midwest and Texas in America. Emigration to Texas came mostly from the places indicated in italics.

Hradec Králové

Horní Čermná

Vysoké Mýto Ústí N.
Chrudim
Čáslav Litomyšl Orlicí

Svitavy

Havlíčkův
Brod
Ždár N.
Sázavou *Hradnice* *Frenštát P.*
Polná *Radhoštěm*
Jihlava The Czech-Moravian
Highlands *Vsetín*

Brno

Třebíc

Hrotovice

Frýdek Místek

Znojmo

Bratislava

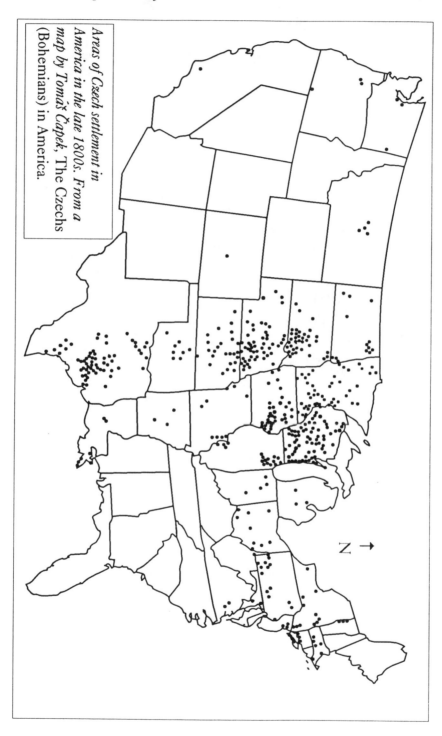

Areas of Czech settlement in America in the late 1800s. From a map by Tomáš Čapek, The Czechs (Bohemians) in America.

Appendix C
Tables

Table 1 Requests for Immigration

Requests made in Dolní Hořice near Chotiny to the district office, October 29, 1858, OU Tabor, k. 164, rg. 4/1/13. Age, Employment, and a Support from Relatives of Emigrants from the Milevsko Region, the Písek District, 1867–1881 (names with + were linked to those settled in Nebraska)

	Age	Employment	Journey paid for or supported by relatives/friends
Jose Rosol	14	*čeledín*	yes
Hynek Nikodým	26	renter	
František Čítek	48	laborer	yes
Jan Kazimour	35	—	
Josef Domín	17	—	yes
František Klíma+	54	—	
František Papač	43	laborer	yes
Václav Křížek	41	mill-hand	
Václav Macháček	44	blacksmith	
Josef Cunát	21	*čeledín*	yes
Václav Šindelář+	17	*čeledín*	yes
František Kotrba	59	*výměnkář*	
Josef Kotrba	49	cottager	
Josef Šedivý	16	laborer	yes
Josef Bouška	18	—	yes
František Bouška	15	—	yes
Josef Veselý	19	—	yes
Jan Kašpar	19	laborer	yes
Jan Matuška	42	laborer	yes
Jan Kálal	35	farmer	
Jan Blažek	21	son of a cottager	yes
Josef Kotrba	41	laborer	yes
Jan Matuška	24	laborer	yes
František Tříska	38	laborer	
Josef Klicman	30	son of a cottager	
Josef Panoch	44	peasant	yes

Table continued

	Age	Employment	Journey paid for or supported by relatives/friends
Adolf Vávra	—	worker	
František Ševčík	36	constr. worker	
Antonín Honsa	16	tailor hand	
Václav Černý	25	—	yes
Václav Jakoubek	45	cottager	
Michal Míka	59	tailor apprentice	
Anna Štastná	22	maid	yes
Jan Ondráček	30	laborer	yes
Bernard Rubín	11	—	yes
Josef Král+	65	laborer	yes
Karel Kofroň	27	laborer	yes
František Tříska+	20	—	
Václav Čurín	19	—	yes
František Hlavín	25	*čeledín*	yes
Barbara Lipová	24	maid	yes
Josef Lipa	15	*čeledín*	yes
Jan Lipa	17	*čeledín*	yes
Jan Pilař	51	laborer	yes
Jan Šíp	43	constr. apprentice	yes
Josefa Smržová	33	—	
Jan Kasal	34	weaver	yes
Jan Lutovský	34	laborer	yes
František Lutovský	28	carpenter	yes
Josef Matějíček	31	laborer	yes
Matěj Lutovský	28	laborer	yes
Jan Bárta+	45	*celedín*	yes
Jan Dušek+	32	laborer	yes

Source: Milevsko, OA Písek, poboc. Mirovice, fond OU Milovice
Note: Most people listed emigrated with families.

Table 2 Applicants for Emigration

Applicants for Emigration in the Písek District (by Occupation and by Age) (1867–1881):

Occupation	Age 10–20	21–30	31 and older
čeledín	3	2	1
renter		1	
laborer	2	4	8
mill-hand			1
blacksmith			1
výměnkář			1
cottager			2
farmer			1
cottager's son		2	
peasant			1
construction worker		1	
tailor hand	1		
tailor apprentice		1	
maid		2	
construction apprentice		1	
weaver			1
carpenter		1	
total	6	12	20

Source: Milevsko, OA Písek, poboc. Mirovice, fond OU Milovice.

Table 3 Czech Population Growth in Nebraska

The Growth of Czech Population in Saunders, Butler, Saline, Colfax, Douglas, Knox, and Howard Counties, 1880 and 1900, and as a Percentage of all Foreign Born:

		1880			1900	
County	N	Czechs	%	N	Czechs	%
Saunders	5,083	1,738	34.2	5,437	1,178	21.7
Saline	3,631	1,627	44.8	3,608	1,885	52.2
Colfax	2,539	1,054	41.5	3,113	1,728	55.5
Butler	2,011	756	37.6	2,900	1,291	44.5
Douglas	12,138	671	5.5	32,244	3,348	10.4
Knox	932	400	42.9	2,784	567	20.4
Howard	1,690	273	16.2	2,715	341	12.6
total	28,024	6,519		52,801	10,338	

Note: N=Total foreign born.

Sources: U.S. Census Office, *Tenth Census: 1880. Population*, p. 519; U.S. Census Office, *Twelfth Census: 1900. Population*, pp. 768–769.

Table 4 Czech Population Growth in Nebraska

Czech Population as a Percentage of the Total Population in Saunders, Butler, Saline, Colfax, Douglas, Knox, and Howard Counties, 1880 and 1900.

	1880		1900	
County	N	%	N	%
Saunders	15,810	11.0	22,085	5.3
Saline	14,491	11.2	18,252	10.3
Colfax	6,588	16.0	11,211	15.4
Butler	9,194	8.2	15,703	8.2
Douglas	37,645	1.8	140,590	2.4
Knox	3,666	10.9	14,343	4.0
Howard	4,391	6.2	10,343	3.3

Note: N=Total population

Sources: U.S. Census Office, *Tenth Census: 1880. Population*, p. 519; U.S. Census Office, *Twelfth Census: 1900. Population*, pp. 768–769.

Table 5 Birth Places

Birth Places of Czechs, Moravians, and Swedes in Selected Townships in Saunders and Saline Counties.

Target Townships (# of cases)	direct route (%)		
	Czechs	Moravians	Swedes
Elk (87)	90% (78)	100% (58)	-
Newman (55)	98% (54)	100% (28)	100% (1)
Bohemia (92)	97% (89)	-	-
Chester (50)	84% (42)	100% (12)	-
Mariposa (4)	100% (4)	-	80% (89)
Chapman (49)	94% (46)	100% (9)	92% (33)
Pleasant Hill (60)	85% (51)	-	100% (1)

Source: U.S.Census Office, *Population Schedules of the Nebraska State Census of 1885.*

Table 6 Common Passages

Most Common Passages Followed by The Sample of Immigrants (Czechs and Swedes)

	Frequency			
State	Czechs	%	Swedes	%
New York	1	3%	-	-
New Jersey	1	3%	-	-
Pennsylvania	2	6%	2	7%
Ohio	7	21%	-	-
Indiana	-	-	1	3%
Michigan	-	-	4	14%
Illinois	6	18%	14	48%
Wisconsin	6	18%	1	3%
Minnesota	-	-	1	3%
Missouri	1	3%	1	3%
Iowa	9	27%	5	17%
total	33	100%	29	100%

Source: Source: U.S. Census Office, *Schedules of the Nebraska State Census of 1885.*

Table 7 Crop Diversification

Crop Diversification by Origin (Entire Population)			
country of origin	mean	standard deviation	# of cases
Bohemia	3.7555	1.8176	364
Great Britain	2.9231	1.8120	39
Germany	2.6825	1.9162	63
Moravia	4.0114	1.8414	88
Scandinavia*	2.6826	1.7428	167
United States	2.4113	1.7041	355

*Sweden, Norway

Source: U.S. Census. *Agricultural Schedules of 1885 Nebraska Census.*

Table 8 Crop Diversification

Crop Diversification by Origin in Seven Townships in Saunders and Saline Counties

# of crops / Origin of population	0	1	2	3	4	5	6	7	Population (total) %
Bohemia	45	13	19	28	103	118	36	2	364
	12.4	3.6	5.2	7.7	28.3	32.4	9.9	0.5	33.8
Gr. Britain	8	1	2	11	12	2	3	-	39
	20.5	2.6	5.1	28.2	30.8	5.1	7.7	-	3.6
Germany	15	6	4	10	17	9	2	-	63
	23.8	9.5	6.3	15.9	27.0	14.3	3.2	-	5.9
Moravia	7	6	5	7	17	29	16	1	88
	8.0	6.8	5.7	8.0	19.3	33.0	18.2	1.1	8.2
Scandinavia	31	18	18	34	39	26	1	-	167
	18.6	10.8	10.8	20.4	23.4	15.6	0.1	-	15.5
U.S.A.	74	39	59	79	71	21	11	1	355
	20.8	11.0	16.6	22.3	20.0	5.9	3.1	0.3	33.0
Total	180	83	107	169	259	205	69	4	1076
	16.7	7.7	9.9	15.7	24.1	19.1	6.4	0.4	100%

For example, to understand the above table: Out of the total of 355 U.S. born in the sample (33% of the total population), 74 did not grow any crops (20.8% of the U.S. population); 39 grew one crop (11.0%), etc.

Table 9 Foreign-born Czech Population in Iowa

Czech Population in the United States, Iowa, and Linn County:				
Year	Country of Birth	No. in USA	No. in Iowa	No. in Linn Co.
1870	Bohemia	40,289	6,766	1,780
1880	Bohemia	85,361	10,554	2,166
1890	Bohemia	118,106	10,928	3,327
1990	Bohemia	156,999	10,809	3,198

Source: *Iowa's Journal of History and Politics*, published by the Historical Society of Iowa, Iowa City, Iowa (April 1944, 42, No.2), and in the study "The Czechs in Cedar Rapids: by Martha E. Griffith (Part 2, July 1944) in *Panorama: A Historical Review of Czechs and Slovaks in the United States of America* (Cicero, Illinois: the Czechoslovak National Council of America, 1970), 40.

Appendix D
Pronunciation Guide

Based on Šara, Milan, Šarová Jitka, and Bytel, Antonín, *Čeština pro cizince* (Praha: Státní pedagogické nakldatelství, 1969)

Czech spelling is far more phonetic than English but it has kept some historical peculiarities which are not phonetic. There are five vowels in Czech. Unlike those in English, they are always pronounced, even in the unstressed or final positions. All Czech vowels can be either short or long.

Short vowels:

a   as in *cup*
o   as in *not*
u   as in *book*
e   as in *set*
i, y   as in *sit*

Long vowels (˙ čárka in Czech):

á   as in *father*
ó   as in *lawn*
ú, ů   as in *stool*
é   no equivalent in English; except for the length it is the same as short e
í, ý   as in *seat*

Unlike English vowels, Czech vowels may all be short or long, whether stressed or unstressed.

Some Czech consonants closely resemble the corresponding English consonant digraphs in sound. The only difference is in spelling:

č   (ˇ háček in Czech) as in *child*
š   as in *ship*
ž   as in *rouge*

Háček is also used over e for the sound [j] after b, p, v, f.

The consonant letters b, v, d, z, m, n, f, s represent the same phonetic values in Czech as they do in English.

The following consonant letters represent different phonetic values in Czech than in English:

c   as in *oats* (thus, Václav [Vatslav] Havel)
g   as in *good* (never as in *general*)
j   as in *you*
ch   no equivalent sound in English. In Czech it is a voiceless sound formed by air passing between the raised back of the tongue and the soft palate. In Czech ch is one letter.
p   as in *pie* (but no aspiration)
t   as in *token* (as above)
k   as in *caliber* (as above)
r   as a "rolled" sound and far more energetic than the English r
l   as in *leave*
h   as in *have*

The following Czech consonants do not exist in English:

ď   as in *duty*
ť   as in *Tuesday*
ň   as in *new*
ř   is produced by the tip of the tongue which vibrates against the upper teeth

The stress in Czech falls on the first syllable of the word.

Footnotes

Introduction

1. Articles in the major newspapers *Národní listy* (*National Papers*), *Česká politika* (*Czech Politics*), *Hlas národa* (*The Voice of the Nation*), *Posel z Prahy* (*The Messenger from Prague*), *Pražský denník* (*Prague's Daily*), published in Bohemia in the second half of the nineteenth century and collected in "Scrapbooks" in Náprstek's collection in Prague, reflect the attitudes different segments of the society held towards the emigration. The material contained in the "Archives of Czechs and Slovaks Abroad" at the University of Chicago have two types of pamphlets published in the Czech lands; one group discouraged would-be emigrants, the other provided (often rosy) information about North America.

2. Mack Walker, *Germany and the Emigration*, 1816–1885 (Cambridge, Mass.: Harvard University Press, 1974), 69.

3. The Austrian emigration statistics are kept in both the German archives and in the Vienna Archive, but the clerks who kept the records often did not distinguish between the different nationalities of the Austro-Hungarian Empire.

4. Esther Jerabek, ed., "Letters to Bohemia: A Czech Settler Writes from Owatonna, 1856–1858," *Minnesota History* 43 (4 Winter 1972), 141.

5. Ethnic institutions are glimpsed through periodical pamphlets published by shipping agent Josef Pastor from Bremen, *České Osady v Americe* (*Czech Settlements in America*) and of articles in newspaper *Pokrok Západu* (*The Progress of the West*) (1879–1890), published in Omaha. The 1885 *Federal Census of Nebraska* is another useful source of information about Czech settlers. An in-depth study of two rural counties with the highest concentration of Czech settlers between 1891 and 1895—Saunders and Saline—helped to define the economic and social character of the Czech farms in Nebraska. *Nebraska, Kansas Czech Settlers, 1891–1895*, and the *Agricultural Census Manuscripts* for 1885 for Nebraska provided the data for this closely focused study.

Chapter 1

1. Brigitte Ogden, "Emigrationen fran Norden till Nordamerika under 1800–talet: Aktualla Forskningsuppgifter," *Historisk Tidsskrift* (Stockholm), 83 (1963):276; Quoted in Jon Gjerde, *From Peasants to Farmers* (Cambridge: Cambridge University Press, 1985), 1. This idea was first expressed by Frank Thistlewaithe in Stockholm, 1960. (See bibliography page 53.)

2. Ludmila Kárníková, *Vývoj obyvatelstva v českých zemích, 1754–1914* (Praha: Academia, 1965), 281.

3. Otto Urban, *Československé dějiny, 1848–1914. I. Hospodářský a sociální vývoj* (Praha: Státní pedagogické nakladatelství, 1988), 22.

4. Ibid., 23.

5. Otto Urban, *Česká společnost, 1848–1914* (Praha: Svoboda, 1982), 293.

6. For an illuminating discussion of the social and economic implications of industrialization for Czech agriculture during this period, see Otto Urban's *Československé dějiny 1848–1914. I. Hospodářský a sociální vývoj* (*History of Czechoslovakia 1848–1914. I. Economic and social growth*).

7. Ibid., 53.

8. Ibid., 55.

9. Ibid., 111.

10. Ibid., 57.

11. Ibid., 55.

12. H. Boker and F. W. von Bulow, *The Rural Exodus in Czechoslovakia: Studies on Movements of Agricultural Population* (Geneva: International Labor Office, 1935), 40.

13. Urban, *Československé dějiny 1848–1914*, 110.

14. Ibid., 56.

15. Ibid., 110.

16. Ibid.

17. Ibid.

18. Ibid., 111.

19. Ibid.

20. Ibid.

21. Ibid., 26.

22. Ibid.

23. Ibid., 24.

24. Kárnáková, *Vývoj obyvatelstva v českých zemích, 1754–1914*, 281.

25. Ibid.

26. Ibid., 282.

27. Ibid., 283.

28. *Československá vlastivěda, Řada II. Národopis* (Praha: Sfinx, 1936), 803.

29. Ibid., 31.

30. Ibid.

31. Kárníková, *Vývoj obyvatelstva v českých zemích*, 283.

32. Ibid., 284.

33. *Československá vlastivěda*, 12.

34. Ibid.

35. Ibid., 32.

Chapter 2

1. U.S. Congress, Senate, U.S. Immigration Commission, 61st Cong., 3rd Session, December 5, 1910–March 4, 1911, Senate Documents, Vol. 12, *Emigration Conditions in Europe* (Washington: Government Printing Office, 1911), 351.

2. Otto Urban, *Československé dějiny 1848–1914. I. Hospodářský a sociální vývoj* (Praha: Státní pedagogické nakladatelství, 1988), 26.

3. Antonín Zavadil, *Kutnohorsko slovem i obrazem*, II volume (Kutná Hora, 1912), 94.

4. Jaroslava Hoffmannová, *Vystěhovalectví z Polné do Severní Ameriky ve druhé polovině XIX. století* (Havlíčkův Brod: Vysočina, 1969), 12.

5. Rudolf Radous "Z počátků škrobárenského průmyslu v Polné," *Vlastivědný sborník Vysočiny III Krajské muzeum v Jihlavě* (Jihlava 1959): 254–255.

6. "Serial o kutnohorských městech a obcích," *Úder* XXI (2, 1.10.1980): 3. Kutná Hora District Archive.

7. *Dějiny okresu Kutná Hora*, 18. Kutná Hora District Archive.

8. Jitka Melicharová, *Kutnohorsko a Střední Polabí. Turistický průvodce ČSSR* (Praha: Olympia, 1969), 22.

9. Josef Pohl, *Vylidňování venkova v Čechách v období 1850–1930* (Praha: Masarykova akademie práce, 1932), 66.

10. Marie Kapavíková, et al., *Kutnohorsko* (Středočeské nakladatelství a knihkupectví Praha, 1978), 16.

11. *Dějiny okresu Kutná Hora*, 18.

12. František Dvorský, *Vlastivěda moravská. II. Místopis. Hrotovský okres* (Brno: Musejní spolek, 1916), 137. Hilly relief of the area, rising up to 500 meters with few flat lands and few meadows are the dominant features of the area. For example, according to a chronicle of the village of Velký Lomeč in the Kutná Hora region, an area west of the area in focus, the fields there had stones that were constantly dug up during plowing and needed melioration. The former district of Čáslav had 38,883 hectares. 61.9% of the area was arable land, meadows 6%, vegetable gardens 0.1% and fruit gardens 2%, graze land 3.5%, forests 20.7%, lakes 9.6%, and non-land was 5.%.

13. Pohl, *Vylidňování venkova v Čechách v období 1850–1930*, 65.

14. Melicharová, *Kutnohorsko a Střední Polabí. Turistický průvodce ČSSR*, 13.

15. *Výsledky šetření (Agrární anketa) poměrů hospodářských i kulturních zemědělského obyvatelstva v království českém v letech 1898–1900. Z původních prací vyšetřujících komisařů* (Praha: Zemědělska rada pro království české, 1914), I.

16. Dvorský, *Vlastivěda moravská*, 22.

17. A letter by František Zpěvák from Zbirov, Bohemia, from November 13, 1881, to *Pokrok Západu* X (54, Dec. 1881): 5. Knihovna Náprstkova muzea.

18. *Okresní úřad Čáslav, 1855–1945 (1948) - inventář*. District Archive in Kutná Hora, Kutná Hora, no date, 4.

19. Lubomir Vaněk and Marie Kapavíková, *Průvodce po archivních fondech a sbírkách* (Kutná Hora: Okresní archív, 1969), 10.

20. *Anketa*, 135.

21. Rudolf Franěk, *Některé problémy sociálního postavení rolnictva v Čechách na konci 19. a počátku 20. století, Rozpravy Československé akademie věd, Řada společenských věd, Ročník 77, sešit 6* (Praha: Academia, 1967), 12.

22. Pohl, *Vylidňování venkova v Čechách v období 1850–1930*, 65. The town of Oporany in Bechyně region in southern Bohemia, farmstead of 9.68 hectares (24.13 acres) was divided into seventy segments. The peasants' debt grew and cases of distrainer's sale of a piece of land or of an estate were common.

23. *Anketa*, 152.

24. Pamětní kniha, obec Velký Lomeč, 12. District Archive in Kutná Hora.

25. Rudolf Franěk, *Některé problémy sociálního postavení rolnictva v Čechách na konci 19. a počátku 20. století*, 23. Majority of farmers' holdings in the region of Kutná Hora were classified into a category of up to ten hectares. Most holdings were less than five hectares within this ten-hectare group. Eighty-two percent of all agricultural enterprises were within this category and it was spread over only 38% of all land available. Estates over thirty hectares were 2.15% and stretched on 25.83% of land.

26. Pohl, *Vylidňování venkova v Čechách v období 1850–1930*, 75.

27. *Anketa*, 136. In the district of Čáslav the large estates which had over one hundred and fifteen hectares of land grew fourfold between 1882 and 1900, and in the district of Kutná Hora, fivefold.

28. *Čeledínská knížka*. Issued in the village of Slatina on 29th of March, 1885. The book belonged to Bartoloměj Flaštín, born Slatina near Klatovy. In possession of Elmer Kral, Grand Island.

29. Ibid., 8.

30. Ibid., 4.

31. Václav Průcha, et al., *Hospodářské dějiny Československa v 19. a 20. století* (Praha: nakladatelství Svoboda, 1974), 33.

32. *Čeledínská knížka*, 3.

33. *Anketa*, 154.

34. Dvorský, *Vlastivěda moravská*, 22.

35. Pohl, *Vylidňování venkova v Čechách v období 1850–1930*, 75.

36. Průcha, et al., *Hospodářské dějiny Československa v 19. a 20. století*, 39.

37. *Anketa*, 137.

38. Pamětní kniha, obec Velký Lomeč, 12.

39. *Anketa*, I.

40. Ibid., XXXIV. Each region was equal to the size of four administrative districts. The surveyors chose four "typical" villages for a detail analysis.

41. Ibid., 8.

42. Ibid., 128.

43. Ibid., 8.

44. Ibid., 161.

45. Pamětní kniha, obec Velký Lomeč, 13.

46. František Lom, "Vývoj a význam zemědělského tisku v procesu zavádění racionální zemědělské výroby v českých zemích do roku 1914," *Vědecká práce Zemědělského muzea* 25 (1985), 15.

47. *Anketa*, IX.

48. *Československá vlastivěda. Řada II. Národopis* (Praha: Sfinx, 1936), 254.

49. Ibid., 255.

50. An exhibit in a farm museum in Přerov nad Labem. An observation during a visit to the museum in July, 1987.

51. Pamětní kniha, obec Velký Lomeč, 13.

52. *Anketa*, 107.

53. Exhibit in Přerov nad Labem.

54. *Československá vlastivěda*, 256.

55. Franěk, *Některé problémy sociálního postavení rolnictva v Čechách na konci 19. a počátků 20. století*, 70.

56. *Sedmnáctá zpráva o činnosti českého odboru rady zemědělské pro Království české za rok 1908* (Praha: Rolnická tiskárna a nakladatelství, 1909), 454–455.

57. *Československá vlastivěda*, 254.

58. Ibid., 255.

59. Ibid.

60. *Anketa*, 128.

61. Ibid., IX.

62. Ibid., 154. The Kutná Hora district had a high rate of one-parent families.

63. Author's personal correspondence, January 10, 1989.

64. *Anketa*, 156.

65. Lom, "Vývoj a význam zemědělského tisku v procesu zavádění racionální zemědělské výroby v českých zemích do roku 1914," 15.

66. *Anketa*, XV.

67. Ibid., 153.

68. Pohl, *Vylidňování venkova v Čechách v období 1850–1930*, 64.

69. Vaněk and Kapaváková, *Průvodce po archivních fondech a sbírkách*, 10. Kutná Hora had an annual quarter-of-a-percent population decrease since 1880.

70. *Československá vlastivěda*, 198.

71. Author's personal correspondence, January 2, 1989.

72. James Denney, "The Homeland Left Behind," *Magazine of the Midlands*, 5 March 1989, 11–15.

73. František Dvorský, *Vlastivěda moravská*, 31.

74. Ibid., 135.

75. Ibid., 19.

76. *Dějiny okresu Kutná Hora*, 19.

77. Dvorský, *Vlastivěda moravská*, 161. Seventy-five % of the church clubs in Kutná Hora region were Catholic, 13% Czech Protestant, and 6% were Protestant of an Evangelic denomination. According to the census from 1910,

for example, in Kutná Hora there were 14,125 Catholics, 335 Protestants, 57 Augustines, 201 Jews, 14 people had "other" faith and 11 no faith out of the total population of the town which was 15,542. In the village of Velký Lomeč 67% were Catholic, 30.5% were Czech Protestants, and 2.5% were Czech Brethren, living together in harmony, according to a chronicle of the village.

78. *Československá vlastivěda*, 269.

79. Ibid., 271.

80. Ibid., 272.

81. Ibid., 276.

82. Ibid., 275.

83. Ibid., 277.

84. Ibid., 298.

85. Dějiny okresu Kutná Hora, 16.

86. Dvorský, Vlastivěda moravská, 19.

87. Anketa, 69.

88. Jaroslav Purš., ed., *Počátky českého národního obrození. Společnost a kultúra v 70. až 90. letech 18. stoleti* (Praha: Academia , 1990), p 170–173.

Chapter 3

1. "Vystěhovalci do Ameriky," *Katolické listy* (15 March 1903), Čechové mimo vlast, 415. Náprstek Collection.

2. Kenneth Miller, *The Czechoslovaks in America* (New York: George H. Doran Company, 1922), 45.

3. Robert I. Kutak, *The Story of a Bohemian-American Village. A Study of Social Persistence and Change* (New York: Columbia University Library, 1933; repr., New York: Arno Press, 1970), 12 (page is to reprint edition).

4. Jiří Kořalka and Květa Kořalková, "Tchecoslovaquie. Basic Features of Mass Emigration from the Czech Lands During the Capitalist Era, 1980," TMs [photocopy], 507.

5. Jan Auerhan, Jan Hejret, and Alois Svojsík, *Anketa o českém vystěhovalectí uspořádaná zahraničním odborem národní rady české* (Praha: Nákladem Národní rady české, 1912), 4.

6. Auerhan, *Anketa*, 7.

7. Jon Gjerde, *From Peasants to Farmers*. The author deals with the conflict between the state religion and pietistic beliefs in Norway that found much support among the rural population. This conflict was an important consideration for emigrants to leave for the United States. An example of Germans leaving their homeland for purely religious reasons is Robert O. Forster, *Zion on Mississippi. The Settlement of the Saxon Lutherans in Missouri, 1839–1841*. The Czechs had a strong rationalist background that is closer analyzed by Kenneth

D. Miller, *The Czecho-Slovaks in America*, by Tomáš Čapek in *The Cechs (Bohemians) in America*, and discussed by Bruce Garver in an article "Czech-American Freethinkers on the Great Plains," in *Ethnicity on the Great Plains*, ed. Frederick C. Luebke, 147–169.

8. Pamětní kniha, obec Velký Lomeč, 1923, 13. District Archive, Kutná Hora, 1850–1945.

9. Jan Fořt, *O stěhování se lidu našeho do ciziny* (Praha: J. Otto, 1876), 37.

10. Auerhan, *Anketa*, 7.

11. "Vystěhovalci," *České noviny* 56 (6 March, 1880), Náprstek Collection, Čechové mimo vlast, IV, 189.

12. OÚ (Town Office) Tábor, Seznam vystěhovalců, k. 86.

13. OÚ Tábor, prez., kanc. hlas. OH from January 20, 1852, and February 26, 1852, k. 1.

14. OÚ Tábor, prez., no. 63/1853, k. 1.

15. E. Barborová, "Vytěhovalectví do Ameriky v Táborském kraji v letech 1855-1862," *Jihočeský sborník historický* XXXV (1966), 28. Between 1853 and 1859, 499 persons left the district. In 1853, 21 families left (altogether 115 people). In the following year 52 families emigrated, four did not have children, six were single which amounted to 282 persons. The rate of emigration accelerated when 102 families left in 1855.

16. E. Barborová, "Vytěhovalectví do Ameriky z Táborském kraji v letech 1855-1862," 28.

17. OÚ Tábor, Žádosti o vystěhovalectí, k.164.

18. Žádost J. Pejši from August 19, 1860, and a protocol from August 21, 1860, OÚ Tábor, k. 165, 4/2/59.

19. Milevsko, OA (District Archive) Písek, poboč. Mirovice, fond OÚ Mil., k.35, 1879.

20. f. OÚ Mil., k. 35, 4/2/1467. Assoc., 1870.

21. Milevsko, OA Písek, poboč. Mirovice, fond OÚMil., k.35, 4/2/431.

22. Ibid.

23. Eleanor E. Ledbetter, *The Czechs of Cleveland* (Cleveland: Americanization Committee, 1919), 8. The Czechs and the Slovaks Living Abroad, Special Collection, University of Chicago Archives [1272]. An investigation of archival records for 1860–1880 of a locality in southern Bohemia revealed that the migration from this area had a familial character which suggests the early Czech rural emigration was not a movement of the poor or destitute, but of those who stood to lose by staying.

24. František Beneš, "Čechové v okresu Manitowoc, Wisconsin, od roku 1847–1932," 83. Czechs and Slovaks living abroad, Special Collection, University of Chicago Archives.

25. Milevsko, OA Písek, poboč. Mirovice, fond OÚ Tábor, k. 165, 4/2/96, 1867.

26. For example, Zdenka Rypka, Czech. MS Collection, Box 1. A letter by Frank Kostlán, Linn County, written on 26 December 1863. IHRC, St. Paul, Minnesota.

27. Letter to the Governor in Prague, from the senate commissioner for the foreign affairs of Bremen, 11 September 1869. Admin. Reg. F 15/1 folium 106r–117r, Vienna Archive.

28. Auerhan, *Anketa*, 10.

29. Letter to the Ministry of foreign Affairs from the Austro-Hungarian consulate in New Orleans, 19 February 1871. 22/10/V. 2 F15, Aus u. Einwanderung 1870–79, Auswanderung 1880–1918, 1/1-15, fol.1-64, 25/IV 31. I/ 38a akten von 1870 bis 1879. Vienna Archive.

30. "Father Franz Prachař in Bremen," *St. Raphael-Blatt* XXVI (3, 1911). Veroffentlichungen aus dem Staatsarchiv der Freien Hansestadt Bremen, 2-P.8.B.8.c.2.b.Bd.2 Nr.36). Not all steamship agencies were unscrupulous and dishonest. Some even had essentially (or at least partially) altruistic missions. To cite one example, the Agency of St. Raphael arranged the transportation of Catholic emigrants from southern Germany and Bohemia to Catholic settlements in the United States on board the ships of the Norddeutsche Loyd steamship company based in Bremen. The St. Raphael agency, founded in 1868 by Peter Paul Cahensly, originally recruited German Catholic emigrants. Towards the turn of the century, German emigration declined, and the St. Raphael network spread to cover areas inhabited by Catholic Poles, Czechs, Slovaks, Ruthenians, Slovenes, and Croatians. St. Raphael agents were posted in Prague and in Bremen to make sure that the Catholic emigrants would not be contacted by "false" agents and by disreputable women.

31. Jiří Kořalka and Květa Kořalková, "Tchecoslovaquie. Basic Features of Mass Emigration From the Czech Lands During the Capitalist Era, 1980(?)," 506.

32. Letter by the regional governor, December 3, 1856, the district police administration records, Kutná Hora, No. 44. Kutná Hora District Archive.

33. Milevsko, OA Písek, poboč. Mirovice, fond OÚ Mil., k.36, 4/2/1789.

34. f. V. Vančata from Vesteč, k.36, 4/2/1540

35. Milevsko, OA Písek, poboč. Mirovice, fond OÚ Tábor, k.165, 4/2/89, 1867.

36. Pamětní kniha, obec Velký Lomeč, 13.

37. Milevsko, OA Písek, poboč. Mirovice, fond OÚ Tábor, k.165, 4/2/97, 1867.

38. Robert Kutnar, *Počátky hromadného vystěhovalectí z Čech v období Bachova absolutismu* (Rozpravy Československé Akademie věd), no. 74, sešit 15. (Praha: ČSAV, 1964), 32.

39. Fořt, *O stěhování lidu našeho do ciziny*, 10.

40. Letter to the Secretary of State Seward from charge d' affaire of Austria in Washington Frankenstein, 16 January 1868, Admin. Reg. F 15/1 folium 106r–117r. Vienna Archive.

41. Report of Austro-Hungarian Consulate in Chicago on emigration, 1892. Admin. Reg. f 15/1 folium 106r–117r. Vienna Archive. For example, from the total of emigrants from Austro-Hungarian empire to the United States in 1892 which was 374,741, the report from the consulate in Chicago reads 180,638 unemployed (women and children included), 104,348 laborers, 28,612 workers in agriculture, and a broad spectrum of jobs follows.

42. Auerhan, *Anketa*, 8.

43. "Vystěhovalci do Ameriky," *Katolické Listy* (15 March 1903), 415.

44. Fořt, *O stěhování lidu našeho do ciziny*, 21.

45. Josef Polišenský, ed., *Začiatky českej a slovenskej emigrácie do USA* (Bratislava: SAV, 1970), 34.

46. Auerhan, *Anketa*, 7.

47. Polišenský, *Začiatky českej a slovenskej emigrácie do USA*, 35.

48. Eva Cironisová, "Vytěhovalectví z milevského okresu přéd první světovou válkou," *Jihočeský sborník historický* 49 (1980), 89.

49. Ibid.

50. "Stran stěhování do Ameriky," *Čech* 78 (6 April 1881) Čechové mimo vlast (ČMV), V., 151, Náprstek collection.

51. "Počet vystěhovalců do USA roste," *Národní listy* 130 (30 May, 1880), Čechové mimo vlast, V., 44.

52. "České kolonie v Evropě a v Severní Americe," *Pokrok Západu* (3 March 1880), ČMV IV., 190. Náprstek collection.

53. "Jaké jsou vyhlídky pro vystěhovalce v Americe," *České noviny* 106 (4 May, 1883), ČMV, 33–34.

54. Ibid.,

55. "Výstraha před stěhováním se do Ameriky," *Česká politika*, 291 (22 October 1887), ČMV IX., 363. Baltimore received 3,009 emigrants from Austro-Hungarian Empire. 4,222 Czechs came to New York in 1887. (From the whole of Austro-Hungarian Empire came 19,994 to New York.)

56. O. Doudlebský, "Máme-li stěhovati se do Ameriky," *Rolnické listy* reprinted in České osady v Americe (1889), 165. Czechs and Slovaks living abroad. Special collection, University of Chicago Archives.

57. "O českém vystěhovalectí," *Národní listy* (9 October 1884), ČMV, 279–280. Náprstek collection.

58. Josef Pačas, Schuyler, a letter to *Pokrok Západu* X (7, 1 June 1881), 3.

59. Ibid.

Chapter 4

1. The volume of Czech emigration is difficult to approximate since, according to the Austrian government's definition, an emigrant was a person who decided to leave permanently, the decision he or she certified by signing a document releasing him or her from Austrian citizenship. Thus, crossing borders with only a travel document or illegally without an emigration passport went undocumented, and cases of shipping agents persuading laborers working in Germany on a seasonal contract, or apprentices getting experience to embark on a journey to the United States were common.

2. Jan Wagner, "Američtí Čechové," *Národní Listy* 14 August 1895. Newspapers clippings in collection "Čechové mimo vlast"/Czechs outside the motherland/ vol. 12,306 (further referred to as ČMV, Náprstek Collection), Náprstek Museum Library, Prague. In 1895 there were close to half a million Czechs (including children) born in the United States.

3. After the defeat of Napoleon in 1815, no European power made a bid for domination in Europe during the remainder of nineteenth century (of course, Germany would make such a bid twice in the first half of the 20th century).

4. Stephan Thernstrom, ed., *Harvard Encyclopedia of Ethnic Groups* (Cambridge: Harvard University Press, 1980), s.v. "Czechs" by Karen Johnson Freeze, 263.

5. Jiří Kořalka and Květa Kořalková, "Tchecoslovaquie. Basic Features of Mass Emigration from the Czech lands during the Capitalist Era, 1980," TMs [photocopy], received from the authors, 508.

6. 61st congress, 3d Session, Senate, document No. 756, Reports of the Immigration Commission, *Statistical Review of Immigration, 1820–1910*, distribution of Immigrants, 1850–1900 (Washington: Government Printing Office, 1911). The Immigration commission. Statistical Review of Immigration, 1820–1910, 45. Between 1899 and 1910, 100,189 Czechs and Moravians (1% of the total population) arrived at the shores of the United States.

7. Stephan Thernstrom, ed., *Harvard Encyclopedia of Ethnic Groups*, 263.

8. Josef Polišenský, "Obecné problémy dějin českého vystěhovalectí, 1850-1914," 1987 TMs (photocopy), 16, received from the author. The absolute numbers of Czechs and Moravians living in the United States grew rapidly between 1870 and 1900. In 1870 the United States had 40,000 people born in the Czech lands. By 1880, the number had risen more than twofold to 85,000, and in 1890 there were 215,000 Czechs. At the end of the century there were 357,000 Czechs.

9. U.S. Immigration Commission, *Statistical Review of Immigration, 1820–1910*, 53–57. For example, in 1899, 2,382 Czechs and Moravians left from the Empire, and only 24 from Germany. The numbers rose towards the end of the first decade of the twentieth century, but remained small, amounting to only 503 people during the period 1899–1910. A route to the United States via Russia was followed by 421 Czechs and Moravians in the same year.

10. "Severo-německý Lloyd přes Baltimore za nízké ceny můžete přátele povolati," *Pokrok Západu* (31 August 1881), 18.

11. "Česko-slovanský Dům pro vystěhovalce," ČMV XVII, 41–42.

12. Senate Documents, vol. 66. 61st Congress, 2nd Session, Senate, Document No. 338, *Reports of the Immigrant Commission. Immigrants in Cities. A Study of the Population of Selected Districts in New York, Chicago, Philadelphia, Boston, Cleveland, Buffalo, and Milwaukee.* Vol. I (Washington: Government Printing Office, 1911), 5.

13. Francis Dvornik, *Czech Contributions to the Growth of the United States* (Chicago: Benedictine Abbey Press, 1962), 26. U.S. Immigration Commission. Occupation of Immigrants, 118.

14. Eleanor E. Ledbetter, *The Czechs of Cleveland* (Cleveland: Administration Committee Mayor's Advisory War Committee, 1919), 8.

15. Dvornik, *Czech Contributions to the Growth of the United States*, 43.

16. 61st congress, 2nd Session, Senate, document No. 338, *Reports of the Immigration Commission, Immigrants in Cities. A Study of the Population of Selected Districts in New York, Chicago, Philadelphia, Boston, Cleveland, Buffalo, and Milwaukee* (in two volumes: Vol. I), 514.

17. Ledbetter, *The Czechs of Cleveland*, 8.

18. Rudolf Bubeníček, *Dějiny Čechů v Chicagu* (Chicago, Illinois: R. Mejdrich, 1939), 16.

19. Primus Sobotka, *Za Atlantským oceánem* (Praha: Matice lidu, 1890), 47–51. University of Chicago Archives, Chicago. [6343]

20. Eduard Vojan, *České Chicago. Adresář a Almanach českého obyvatelstva v Chicagu* (Chicago: The Bohemia American Hospital Association, 1915), 30–31. University of Chicago Archives [991].

21. Niles Carpenter, *Immigrants and Their Children* (New York: Arno Press and the New York Times, 1969), 61–63.

22. E. P. Hutchinson, *Immigrants and Their Children 1850–1950.* A Volume in the Census Monograph Series (New York: John Wiley, 1956), 23.

23. U.S. Immigration Commission, *Occupations of Immigrants*, 119.

24. Ibid., 63.

25. Ibid., 8.

26. Ibid., 117.

27. Ibid., 71.

28. Ibid., 75.

29. U.S. Immigration Commission, *Immigrants in Industries*, Part 24: Recent Immigrants in Agriculture, Vol. II, 380.

30. U.S. Immigration Commission, *Immigrants in Cities: Chicago*, 307.

31. Ibid., 315.

32. U.S. Immigration Commission, *Immigrants in Cities: General Tables*, 197.

33. Martha Eleanor Griffith, "The Czechs in Cedar Rapids," *The Iowa Journal of History and Politics* 42 (2 April 1944), 118–120.

34. Carpenter, *Immigrants and Their Children*, 19–20.

35. Věra Láska, ed., *The Czechs in America, 1633–1977*, A Chronology & Fact Book Ethnic Chronology Series, Number 28 (Dobbs Ferry, New York: Oceana Publication, Inc., 1978), 38.

36. U.S. Immigration Commission. *Immigrants in Industries*, Part 24, Recent Immigrants in Agriculture, Vol. II, 376. Some Czechs came to Texas because they had friends already living there. For example, in 1866 Jan Šulák wrote in his application for a permission to emigrate to Texas to *okresní úřad* (district office) in Frenštát: "About eight years ago many of my friends emigrated to North America. They became owners of a great homestead and they live happily in Rostprille. I am an owner of a farmstead in Bordovice and I live well. I have decided that I want to move with my family to the United States in order to join my friends and to improve my future." Source: Appendix to Bača, 6023/ 1225, M3354, Státní okresní archív, Brno, Czechoslovakia.

37. Marion Bergman, "America's Slavic Legacy," Unpublished Manuscript, 1975, 119. Immigration History Research Center, St. Paul, Minnesota, 26c.

38. Dvornik, *Czech Contributions to the Growth of the United States*, 48–49.

39. U.S. Immigration Commission, *Immigrants in Industries*, Part 24: Recent Immigrants in Agriculture, Vol. II, 376.

40. Marion Bergman, "America's Slavic Legacy," 125.

41. Tomáš Čapek, *The Czechs (Bohemians) in America. A Study of Their National, Cultural, Political, Social, Economic and Religious Life* (Boston: 1920; repr., New York: AMS, 1969), 37.

42. Nan Mashek, "Bohemia Farmers in Wisconsin," *Charities* 13 (3 December 1904), 211–215.

43. Beneš-Vyskočil, "Czechs in Manitowoc County, Wisconsin, 1847– 1932," *Immigration History Research Center*, 3.

44. Ferdinand F. Doubrava, "Experience of a Bohemian Emigration Family," *Wisconsin Magazine of History* (1924), 403.

45. Láska, 9.

46. Jan Rosický, *Jak je v Americe?* (Omaha, Nebraska: Národní tiskárny, 1906), 39.

47. Láska, 16.

48. Milan Woodrow Jerabek, "Czechs in Minnesota" (M.A. Thesis, University of Minnesota, 1939), 53.

49. Josef Vondra "Pamětí českých osadníků v Americe," *Kalendář Amerikán* 30 (1907), 276.

50. Panorama, 47.

51. Ibid.

52. Ibid.

53. Ibid.

54. U.S. Immigration Commission, *Immigrants in Industries*, Part 24: Recent Immigrants in Agriculture, Vol. II, 376.

55. Rosický, 40.

56. U.S. Immigration Commission, *Immigrants in Industries*, 376.

57. Martha Eleanor Griffith, "The Czechs in Cedar Rapids," 118–120.

58. Ibid., 122–123.

59. A letter by Josef Kotlán, Linn County, Iowa, December 26, 1863. Zdenka Rypka's Manuscript Collection, Box 1, IHRC, St. Paul, Minnesota.

60. Nan Mashek, "Bohemian farmers in Wisconsin," 214.

61. Ibid.

62. Ibid., 213.

63. "Drobnosti...," *České osady v Americe 3* (1 March 1891), 45.

64. U.S. Immigration Commission, *Immigrants in Industries*, 376.

65. Ibid.

66. Láska, 23.

67. William C. Sherman, ed., "Origins of North Dakota Czech Settlers," in *Plains Folk. North Dakota's Ethnic History* (North Dakota Centennial Heritage Series: Fargo, North Dakota, 1988), 307.

68. Tomáš Čapek, *The Cechs (Bohemians) in America*, 60.

69. Sherman, "Origins of North Dakota Czech Settlers," 306.

Chapter 5

1. U.S. Congress, Senate, U.S. Immigration Commission, *Distribution of Immigrants, 1850–1900*, 535.

2. *Národní listy*, ČMV, 1895, Náprstek Collection.

3. The number was probably higher because Czechs sometimes gave Austria as their country of origin (Bohemia, of course, was not a "country").

4. Population, table 14. Foreign born population, distributed according to country of birth, by states and territories: 1890. Abstract of the eleventh census: 1890. Department of the interior, census division. Second edition, revised and enlarged. (Washington, Government printing office, 1896.)

5. U.S. Congress, Senate, U.S. Immigration Commission, *Distribution of Immigrants*, 535.

6. Lloyd Bernard Sellin, "The Settlement of Nebraska to 1880" (M.A. Thesis, University of South Carolina, 1940), 216.

7. "Popis jednotlivých států a teritorií," *České osady v Americe* 4 (1 April 1889), 250.

8. E. Evelyn Cox, "1870 Nebraska Census," vol. 1 (Ellensberg, Washington: Ancestree House, 1979), 56–78.

9. "Letter," *Pokrok Západu* VII (9, 3 July 1878), 3, Náprstek Collection.

10. Clinto Machan and James W. Mendl, *Krásná Amerika, A Study of the Texas Czechs, 1851–1939* (Austin, Texas: Eakin Press, 1983), 131.

11. They were most likely following their relatives or friends who may have paid their passage.

12. Frank Mareš, Nebraska, *Kansas Czech Settlers, 1891–1895*, comp. by Margie Sobotka (Omaha: Czech Nebraska Historical Society) 115.

13. Walter D. Kamphoefner, *The Westfalians. From Germany to Missouri* (Princeton: Princeton University Press, 1987), 71.

14. Mareš, Nebraska, *Kansas Czech Settlers*, 134.

15. Pamětní kniha obce Kluky. District Archive in Kutná Hora.

16. Rose Rosický, *A History of Czechs (Bohemians) in Nebraska* (Omaha: Czech Historical Society of Nebraska, 1929), 97.

17. Mareš, Nebraska, *Kansas Czech Settlers*. A small number of Czechs who settled with the Moravians came from western Bohemia near Plzeň, the central area of the Klatovy region, and the Kutná Hora region. Only a few Czechs from western Bohemia came to Butler County.

18. Mareš, Nebraska, *Kansas Czech Settlers*.

19. Robert P. Swierenga, "Dutch Patterns of Migration to the United States in the Mid-Nineteenth Century" (St. Paul, Minn.: Immigration History Research Center, 1986), 2, photocopied.

20. Stephan Thernstrom, ed., *Harvard Encyclopedia of Ethnic Groups* (Cambridge: Harvard University Press, 1980), s.v. "Czechs" by Karen Johnson Freeze, 263.

21. Ibid., 263.

22. "Paměti českých osadníků v Americe," *Kalendář Amerikán* 28 (1905), 263–364.

23. Vladimír Kucera, ed., *Czechs and Nebraska* (Lincoln, Nebraska: By the author, 15th & R Sts., 1976), 16. Vodička sponsored most of the campaigns advertising new "excellent" land for farming. He offered trips with picnics to areas in western Nebraska where he had large amounts of land for sale. The editors of *Pokrok Západu* printed favorable letters from satisfied settlers about the joys of life and farming in Nebraska.

24. Rosický, comp., *A History of Czechs (Bohemians) in Nebraska*, 208.

25. V. J. Holeček, "První Čechove na Niobraře," *Kalendář Amerikán* 45 (1922), 232, Náprstek Collection.

26. Josef Holeček, "Dopisy," *Pokrok Západu* (25 October 1876), 2.

27. Ibid.

28. Ibid.

29. Fred A. Shannon, *The Farmer's Last Frontier. Agriculture, 1860–1897* (New York: Rinenart & Co., 1945), 173.

Chapter 6

1. U.S. Immigration Commission, *Immigrants in Industries*, Part 24: Recent Immigrants in Agriculture, Vol. II, 398.

2. Ibid.

3. D. Aidan McQuillan, *Prevailing Over Time, Ethnic Adjustment on the Kansas Prairies, 1875–1925* (Lincoln: University of Nebraska Press, 1990), 13.

4. Ibid., 10–14.

5. Allan G. Bogue, *Money at Interest* (Lincoln, Nebraska: University of Nebraska Press, 1955), 1–2.

6. "Letter," *Pokrok Západu* (3 July 1878), 2. At the time of the highest influx of Czechs and Moravians to Nebraska, the public lands were for sale, up to 160 acres, for $2.50 per acre if the land was next to the railroad. If the land was in an area without the railroad one acre sold for $1.25 in 1886.

7. Bogue, *Money at Interest*, 3.

8. Antonín Tomička, "Zprávy z českých osad," *České osady v Americe*, Special edition (1886).

9. Frank Bureš, "Letter," *České osady v Americe* 4 (1 February 1889), 200.

10. Robert I. Kutak, *The Story of a Bohemian-American Village*. A Study of Social Persistance and Change (New York: Columbia University Library, 1933; repr., New York: Arno Press, 1970), 25.

11. Josef Kastl, "Zprávy z českých osad," *České osady v Americe* 5 (1 October 1891), 158.

12. Walter D. Kamphoefner, *The Westfalians. From Germany to Missouri* (Princeton, New Jersey: Princeton University Press, 1987), 81.

13. Frank Kobl, "Zprávy," *České osady v Americe. Příloha*, 1886.

14. Václav Kříž, "Letters," *České osady v Americe* 2 (1886), 3.

15. Janet Varejcka, "The Czech Immigrant—A Process of Acculturation: Schuyler, Nebraska, 1870–1920" (M.A. Thesis, University of Nebraska at Omaha, 1977), 15.

16. Ibid., 29.

17. "Hlavní kniha domovních listů," 1874–1919, Kniha č.9. Okresní archív Kutná Hora, fond OÚ.

18. V. J. Štědrý, Broken Bow, Custer County, "Letter," *Pokrok Západu* (1 September 1891), 10.

19. Josef Maštalíř, "Zprávy z českých osad," *České osady v Americe* 4 (1 February 1889), 198.

20. J. W. Beran, "Letters," *České osady v Americe* 4 (1 February 1889), 197.

21. *Pokrok Západu* (6 January 1882).

22. Kutak, *The Story of a Bohemian-American Village*. A Study of Social Persistence and Change, 9.

23. Joseph John Van Hoff, "A History of the Czechs in Knox County, Nebraska" (M.A. Thesis, University of Nebraska-Lincoln, 1938), 8.

24. Fr. J. Lepša, "Počátky českých osadníků," *České osady v Americe* 5 (1 January 1891), 4–6.

25. Elsie Haudek, ed., "The History of Frank and Teresia (Chapek) Benes" (Weston, Nebraska: By the author, 1985), 4. P. F. K. Ringsmuth, "Malé české posvícení," *České osady v Americe* 5 (1 October 1891), 183.

26. Fred Shannon, *The Farmer's Last Frontier. Agriculture, 1860–1897* (New York: Rinenart & Co., 1945), 4.

27. Antonín Tomička, "Zprávy z českých osad," Příloha. *České osady v Americe* (1886).

28. "Příloha amerického dělníka," *České osady v Americe* IV (10 March 1889), 223.

29. Pavel Albieri, "U českých farmářů," *Národní Listy* (22 May 1893), 209. ČMV 11.

30. R. Strimpl, "Příloha amerického rolníka," Rolnické listy sedlčanské quoted in *České osady v Americe* 4 (1 March 1889): 223.

31. P. S. Šafařík, "Letters," *České osady v Americe* 4 (15 February 1889), 201.

32. J. W. Beran, "Letters," 197.

33. U.S. Immigration Commission, *Immigrants in Industries*, Part 24: Recent Immigrants in Agriculture, Vol. II, 377.

34. United States, Eighth Census, Agriculture, pp. 172–175; Ninth Census, *Industry and Wealth*, pp. 198–201; Tenth Census, Agriculture, 162, quoted in Lloyd Bernard Sellin, "The Settlement of Nebraska to 1880" (M.A. Thesis, University of South California, 1940), 226.

35. V. Luxa, "Setí lnu," *Hospodář* 3 (1 April 1893), 3.

36. Václav Křičkač, "Letters," ČMV, 240.

37. Josef Novotný, "Počasí. Úroda. Pozemky," *České osady v Americe* 4 (1 February 1889), 199.

38. "Linwood, Butler County. Úroda kukuřice. Neúroda pšenice. Ovoce," *České osady v Americe* 4 (1 February 1889), 196.

39. "Dopisy z českých osad," *České osady v Americe* 5 (1 March 1891), 37.

40. Otopalík, "Drobnosti z českých osad," *České osady v Americe* 5 (1 May 1891), 80.

41. Frank Vlastník, "Chov dobytka," *České osady v Americe* 4 (15 March 1889), 240.

Chapter 7

1. Josef Kostlán to his parents, 26 December 1863, Rypka Collection, Minnesota Immigration History Center, St. Paul.

2. Ibid.

3. Martha E. Griffith, "The Czechs in Cedar Rapids" (Part 2, July 1944), in *Panorama. A Historical Review of Czechs and Slovaks in the United States of America* (Cicero, Illinois: the Czechoslovak National Council of America, 1970), 4.

4. Tomáš Čapek, *The Čechs (Bohemians) in America* (Boston: 1920, repr., New York: AMS, 1949), 46–47.

5. Marcus L. Hansen, "Official Encouragement of Immigration to Iowa," *The Iowa Journal of History and Politics* 19: 159–195, in Martha E. Griffith, 9.

6. Věra Láska, ed., *The Czechs in America, 1633–1977, A Chronology & Fact Book*, Ethnic Chronology Series, Number 28 (Dobbs Ferry, New York: Oceana Publications, Inc., 1978), 11.

7. Martha E. Griffith, "The Czechs in Cedar Rapids," 40.

8. Cyril M. Klimesh, *They Came to This Place. A History of Spillville, Iowa and Its Czech Settlers* (Sebastopol, California: Methodius Press, 1983), 52.

9. Martha E. Griffith, "The History of Czechs in Cedar Rapids, 1852–1942," 4.

10. Klimesh, 103.

11. "Paměti českých osadníků v Americe," *Kalendář Amerikán* 20 (1897), 202.

12. Klimesh, 54.

13. J. J. Král, "Čechové ve Spojených Statech," *Kalendář Amerikán* 28 (1905), 236.

14. "Paměti českých osadníků v Americe," *Kalendář Amerikán* 19 (1896), 192–193.

15. *Panorama. A Historical Review of Czechs and Slovaks in the United States of America* (Cicero, Illinois: the Czechoslovak National Council of America, 1970), 42.

16. Griffith, 7.

17. Klimesh, 53.

18. Ibid., 54.

19. Ibid., 59.

20. Ibid.

21. Ibid., 62.

22. Ibid., 103.

23. Ibid., 102.

24. Ibid., 51.

25. Ibid., 12.

26. Ibid.

27. Ibid., 27.

28. Ibid., 25.

29. Ibid., 189.

30. Láska, ed., *The Czechs in America, 1633–1977*, 37.

31. *Panorama*, 46.

32. AD to Marie Bohdanecká, Čimelice, February 20, 1893. Milan Kuna, Ludmila Bradová, Antonín Čubr, Markéta Hallová, Jitka Slavíková, *Antonín Dvořák, Korespondence a Dokumenty*, Kritické vydani. Sv. 3, 1890–1895 (Praha: Supraphon, 1989), 180.

33. Ibid., 207.

34. Klimesh, 155.

35. Ibid.
36. Kuna, 180.
37. Ibid., 206.
38. Klimesh, 156.
39. Kuna, 193.
40. Ibid., 202.
41. Ibid., 207.
42. Klimesh, 161.
43. Ibid., 164.
44. Klimesh, 160.
45. Ibid., 165.
46. Ibid.
47. Kuna, 194.
48. Klimesh, 157.
49. Kuna, 199.
50. Ibid., 207.
51. Ibid., 206.

Chapter 8

1. Clinton Machan and James W. Mendl, *Krásná Amerika: A Study of the Texas Czechs, 1851–1939* (Austin, Texas: Eakin Press, 1983), 1.
2. Věra Láska, ed., *The Czechs in America, 1633–1977* (Dobbs Ferry, New York: Oceana Publications, Inc., 1978), 7.
3. Machan and Mendl, *Krásná Amerika*, 34–35.
4. Ibid., 2.
5. W. Phil Hewitt, "Czech Texan Immigration and Community, 1850–1900," in *The Czechs in Texas*, A Three-Day Multidisciplinary Symposium sponsored by the Department of English, Texas A&M University, ed. Clinton Machan, Temple, Texas, 1978, 45.
6. "Paměti českých osadníků v Americe," *Kalendář Amerikán* 31 (1908), 297.
7. Tomáš Hruška, "Paměti českých osadníků v Americe," *Kalendář Amerikán* 30 (1907), 266–267.
8. Machan and Mendl, 28.
9. Hewitt, "Czech Texan Immigration and Community, 1850–1900," 44.
10. John T. Kroulik, "The First Group Migrations of Czechs to Texas," *The Czechs in Texas*, 53.
11. "František Branecký v Praze v Texasu," *Kalendář Amerikán* 9 (1886), 189.
12. Kroulik, 53.
13. Hewitt, 45.
14. Kroulik, 57.
15. "Paměti českých osadníků v Americe," *Kalendář Amerikán* 31 (1908), 277–278.
16. "František Branecký v Praze v Texasu," *Kalendář Amerikán* 9 (1886), 189.

17. Tomáš Čapek, *The Cechs (Bohemians) in America* (Boston: -, 1920, repr., New York: AMS, 1969), 49–50.

18. "Paměti českých osadníků v Americe," *Kalendář Amerikán* 35 (1912), 256.

19. Machan and Mendl, 42.

20. Petr Mikeška, "Paměti českých osadníků v Americe," *Kalendář Amerikán* 30 (1907), 257–258.

21. Thadious T. Polasek, "The Early Life of Moravia, Texas," *The Czechs in Texas,* 66.

22. Ibid.

23. Machan and Mendl, 81.

24. Ibid., 82.

25. Jan Rosický, *Jak se zije v Americe?* (Omaha, Nebraska: Národní tiskárny, 1906), 33.

26. Hewitt, 46.

27. Joe Malik, Jr., "The Contributions and Life of the Czechs in Texas," *The Czechs in Texas,* 14–15.

28. Machan and Mendl, 72.

29. R. L. Skrabanek, "Snook, Texas—A Uniqueness in Czech Culture," *Czech Footprints Across the Bluebonnet Fields of Texas,* Proceedings of Second Czech Symposium, 1983, ed. Anjanette Mesecke, Temple Junior College, 66.

30. Ibid., 67.

31. Ibid., 69.

32. Hewitt, 47.

Chapter 9

1. Josef Kostlán to his parents, 1863, 1865, Rypka Collection, Minnesota Immigration History Center.

2. Bruce M. Garver, "Czech-American Freethinkers on the Great Plains, 1871–1914," in *Ethnicity on the Plains,* ed. Frederick C. Luebke (Lincoln, Nebraska: University of Nebraska Press, 1980), 148.

3. Janet Varejcka, "The Czech Immigrant-A Process of Acculturation: Schuyler, Nebraska, 1870–1920" (M.A. thesis, University of Nebraska, 1977), 56–57.

4. Garver, 149.

5. "České osady v Americe," *Národní Listy* (5 July 1894), 36. CMV, 12.

6. L. Šatava, "Čeští vystěhovalci do USA v 19. století a jejich tisk," *Český novinář* 9 (1985), 132.

7. Ibid., 149–150.

8. Clinton Machan and James W. Mendl, *Krásná Amerika: A study of the Texas Czechs, 1851–1939* (Austin, Texas: Eakin Press, 1983), 130.

9. L. Šatava "K problematice formování a stabilizace českého etnika v USA (1848–1914)," 34. MS received from NSHS (David Murphy).

10. Joseph John Van Hoff, "A History of the Czechs in Knox County, Nebraska," 21.

11. Garver, 148.

12. Martha Eleanor Griffith, "The Czechs in Cedar Rapids," The Iowa Journal of History and Politics 42 (2 April, 1944), 56.

13. Ernest Žižka, *Czech Cultural Contributions* (?) IV University of Chicago Archives, Special Collection. [1393]

14. Garver, 148.

15. "Paměti českých osadníků v Americe," *Kalendář Amerikán* (1882–1911).

16. "Poměry českých vystěhovalců ve Spojených státech amerických," *Pokrok Západu* (28 March 1877), 47. ČMV 2.

17. Josef Novotný, "Zprávy z českých osad," *České osady v Americe* 4 (15 March 1889), 239.

18. Francis Dvornik, *Czech Contributions to the Growth of the United States* (Chicago: Benedictine Abbey Press, 1962), 57.

19. "Český kněz v Americe," *Národní listy* (16 December 1979), ČMV 4, 173. Garver, 152.

20. "Paměti českých osadníků v Americe," *Kalendář Amerikán* 29 (1906), 249.

21. Al. Vokoun, "Sebevraždy v našich národních spolcích ČSPS, ČSBJ, Jednota Táboritů," *Hrozná čísla* (Cedar Rapids, Iowa: České bratrstvo v Americe, 1899), 339. CMV 15. The author gave most likely highly exaggerated numbers at one hundred per one thousand annually in the late 1890s by the Czech Brethren.

22. Machan and Mendl, 83.

23. John Runbold Kleinschmidt, "The Political Behavior of the Bohemia and Swedish Ethnic Groups," 206.

24. George Brown Tindall, *America. A Narrative History*, 2d ed. (New York: W.W. Norton & Company), 949.

25. Joe A. Fisher, "The Liquor Question in Nebraska, 1880–1890" (M.A. Thesis, University of Nebraska-Omaha, 1952), 7.

26. "Letter," *Pokrok Západu* 10 (1 June 1881), 2.

27. František Štáva "Letter," *České osady v Americe*, 9 (February 1889), 202.

28. Letter to Josefa Náprstkova, Praha, 11 May 1903, from Charles Kresl, Chicago. American Correspondence, 18–19, Special Collections, Náprstek Collection.

29. Kleinschmidt, 149.

30. Fred A. Shannon, *The Economic History of the United States* (New York: Rinenart & Co., 1945), vol. 5, The Farmer's Last Frontier. Agriculture, 1860–1897, 4.

31. Kleinschmidt, 207.

32. Tindall, 827–828.

33. "Farmerska Alliance," *Pokrok Západu* 10 (9 March 1882), 1.

34. Josef Kastl, "Letter," *České osady v Americe* 5 (1 October 1891), 138.

35. Garver, 158.

36. Machan and Mendl, 97–98.

37. Czech women organized Společnost českých dam (The Society of Bohemian Dames).

38. Interview by the author, May, 1990.

39. Panorama. *A Historical Review of Czechs and Slovaks in the United States of America* (Cicero, Illinois: the Czechoslovak National Council of America, 1970), 42.

40. Ibid.

41. Griffith, 24.

42. V. J. Holeček, "První Čechové na Niobraře," *Kalendář Amerikán* 45 (1922), 248.

43. V. Kašpar, "Dopisy," *Pokrok Západu* 10 (20 December 1881), 3. One of the salient characteristics widely attributed to Czech immigrants was a high level of literacy—supposedly, 98.5 % could read and write. Hence, contemporary observers have suggested that Czechs who came to the United States were well-educated and had an interest in literature and culture. In Texas, the Czechs and Moravians had the reputation of industrious, intelligent, and highly educated people.

44. U.S. Immigration Commission, *Immigrants in Industries*, Part 24: Recent Immigrants in Agriculture, Vol. II, 399.

45. Ibid., 398.

46. Varejcka, 36.

47. A. Z. Donato, "Zprávy z českých osad," *České osady v Americe* 5 (1 October 1891), 139.

48. "Do Crete a okolá," *Pokrok Západu* 2 (18 June 1873), 4.

49. "Jak zrcadlo ukazuje," *Svit* (8 January 1896), 256. CMV 13.

50. Emil Sobota, *U amerických krajanů* (Praha: Edvard Leschinger), 8. Zvláštní otisk z Naší Doby, 36.

51. Oldrich Kašpar, *Tam za mořem je Amerika. Dopisy a vzpomínky českých vystěhovalců do Ameriky v 19. století* (Praha: Československý spisovatel, 1986), 228. Antonín Kříž, "Počátky v Americe," *České osady v Americe* 4 (1 September 1888), 101.

52. J. Štolba, "Za oceánem," *České osady v Americe* 5 (1 January 1891), 4–6.

53. Frank Musil, "Zprávy," *České osady v Americe* 3 (1886).

Glossary

Anketa: A survey ordered by the Assembly of the Kingdom of Bohemia in 1876. Farm producers and local government officials were questioned about the situation in agriculture.

Bohemia: Celtic tribe of the *Boii* (5th century C.C. settled on the territory of the modern Czech republic, and left behind a number of place-names, above all Bohemia, referring to the part or the territory called *"Čechy."*

Čechy: Name from the west Slav tribe *"Čechy."* The Přemysl dynasty had roots in this tribe, which was based in the Prague valley. In the tenth century, the Přemyslids conquered the entire territory populated by the Czechs. Beginning in the eleventh century, Moravia and Silesia were permanently annexed to this territory, the whole of which then came to be called Bohemia.

čeledín: Permanent agricultural worker employed by a farmer.

čeledínská knížka: Passport/contract contained in a book (an identity card with descriptive data such as age, height, weight, and hair color). The *čeledín* had to carry this document at all times.

Češi: The indigenous population of the Czech lands (now numbering 9–10 million). They are the descendants of west Slavic tribes living in the Czech lands since the sixth century. The language spoken is of a west Slavonic variety.

České osady v Americe: Periodical informing prospective emigrants about the conditions and opportunities in the United States. The periodical printed letters of satisfied settlers and was published by Josef Pastor, an agent for a ship company. (The most complete collection is in Náprstek museum, Prague, Czech Republic.)

Česko-Slovanský Podpůrný Spolek (Č.S.P.S.): Czech-Slav Benevolent Association, a fraternal insurance organization founded in 1854. In 1897, the westerners left the C.S.P.S. and formed the **Západní Česká Bratrská Jednota** (Z.C.B.J.— Western Fraternal Life Association).

chalupník (cottager): Peasant; usually did not own horses.

Charles University (Karlova universita): Founded in 1348 by the Holy Roman Emperor Charles IV. It is the oldest university in central Europe, organized into four schools: the School of Philosophy, Medical School, Law School, and School of Theology. The university flourished in the 1380s when it competed for popularity with the university in Paris. In 1882, Karlova universita split into a Czech and a

German school (according to the language used in classes). In 1920, the Czech school was declared Karlova universita, and closed during the German occupation (1939–1945), while the German school continued to exist. In 1945 the latter was closed by a presidential decree.

Czech Brethren: Followers of the Brethren Union, founded in 1457 in Kunvald. They believed in moral purity and pacifism. Persecuted in 1620, many went into exile, mainly to Poland and America.

děvečka: Peasant maid on a farm. She fed and milked cows, took care of poultry and pigs; cleaned the yard. At harvest time she helped in the fields and in the kitchen. She slept in the servant quarters.

Dillingham Commission: Popular name for the reports (published in 1911) of the Immigration Commission, named after the senator serving as chair of the commission. Created in 1907 by an act of the United States Congress. Designed to provide a comprehensive analysis of immigrant peoples and to show the correlation between ethnicity and illiteracy, crime, disease, occupation, income, and other factors.

Habsburg Monarchy: The Habsburg family came from southern Germany. The first Habsburg to become Holy Roman Emperor was elected in the thirteenth century; after 1436 this title became a Habsburg monopoly. The zenith of the Habsburgs' power came in the sixteenth century when Emperor Charles V ascended the Spanish throne. In 1526, his brother Ferdinand became the king of the Czech lands and Hungary and the Duke of Austria; the Austrian Monarchy dates from this time. His successors became the Holy Roman Emperors until 1804. The "dual monarchy" in 1867 gave Hungary autonomy within a newly constituted Austro-Hungarian Empire; the latter lasted only until the end of World War I.

Hospodář (Farmer): An Omaha-based agricultural paper published in the Czech language. (Most issues are in the Archives, Love Library, University of Nebraska, Lincoln.)

Hus, Jan (1372–1415): Czech philosopher, preacher, and leader of a reform movement. In 1400, he became a priest and later served as chancellor of Charles University in Prague. He criticized the high clergy and opposed the Archbishop of Prague. For his refusal to rescind his criticism and his heretical teachings, he was burned at the stake in Kostnice.

Kalendář Amerikán: American Almanac with freethinking bias, published in Chicago. (The most complete collection is in the Archives of the Czechs and Slovaks Abroad, Special Collections, The University of Chicago Library.)

Komenský, Jan Ámos (1592–1670): Czech philosopher, theologian, writer, historian and politician, reformer of pedagogy. In 1628 Komenský emigrated to Poland, and later to England, Sweden, Hungary, and the Netherlands. He was one of the leaders of the Brethren.

Kutná Hora (pop. 21,546): A mining settlement thirty miles east of Prague, established in the second half of the thirteenth century after the discovery of silver there. At the end of that century Kutná Hora became a town. Silver coins were minted there.

malorolník: A landowner who owned 5–25 acres and a small cottage. Tilling of his own and/or rented land was the main source of his livelihood. His work force was his family; he had no hired labor.

Masaryk, Tomáš Garrigue (1850–1937): Czech philosopher, sociologist, and statesman. As a professor at Charles University in Prague and a deputy to the Empire Council in Vienna, Masaryk expressed his views on the question of Czech nationhood. When World War I broke out he fled abroad and became the leader of the anti-Austrian resistance movement. He negotiated Czechoslovakia's independence after the war. Upon his return to Prague at the end of 1918, he was elected the first president of the new Czechoslovak republic.

Moravia: Settled by Slavs in the sixth century and united under Duke Mojmír I by 830, Moravia was the core of the Greater Moravian Empire during the Mojmírovs dynasty. The empire was destroyed by Hungarians in 907. It was the center of the future Czech state when it moved to the Prague valley.

Moravians: Slav population living on the territory of Moravia. Chronicles first mention of Moravians in 822.

Moravské noviny (Moravian News): Occasionally published letters encouraging northern Moravians to emigrate to Texas.

Náprstek, Vojtěch (1826–1894): Czech industrialist. In 1848–58 Náprstek lived in the United States, where he organized activities of Czech-Americans. In 1862, he founded the Czech Industrial Museum of Náprstek in Prague; this museum houses non-European ethnographic collections and a library. Náprstek was a supporter of the woman's emancipation movement.

Národní listy (National Pages): Liberal national paper read mainly by the middle class.

Pokrok Západu (Progress of the West): A weekly Czech-language newspaper founded in 1871 and published in Omaha. (Located in Náprstek museum.)

rolník: Agricultural producer, small *sedlák.*

sedlák: Owner of a medium or large farm (twelve to fifty acres of land).

sokol (falcon): Gymnastic organization founded in Bohemia in 1862 by Miroslav Tyrš and Jindřich Fugner, and based on the idea of harmony between physical and mental development. Within the context of the Austro-Hungarian Empire, *sokol* became a gymnastic organization for the general public, supporting ideas of the national independence movement.

Slovakia: A part of the Great Moravian Empire in the ninth century. In 1018–1918 it was ruled by Hungary; in1918–1938, part of Czechoslovakia; in 1939–1945, an autonomous Slovak republic; in 1946–1992, a part of the Czechoslovak Federative Republic. On January 1, 1993, it became independent.

Slovanská lípa: A patriotic club originating in Bohemia. Established also in America with branches in many midwestern Czech-American communities in the nineteenth century. The various local chapters founded libraries and supported Czech cultural programs.

výměnek: Contractual agreement that guaranteed a pension to the retiring owners of agricultural or other real estate paid by the new title holders (frequently to parents by their children). The guarantee entitled the retirees housing and a pension in kind or in money.

výměnkař: A retired peasant who lived on part of the property (*výměnek*) he had bequeathed to his next of kin.

Selected Bibliography

BOOKS

Balch, Emily Green. *Our Slavic Fellow Citizens*. New York: Charities Publication Committee, 1910.

Barton, Josef J. *Peasants and Strangers: Italians, Rumanians, and Slovaks in an American City, 1890–1950*. Cambridge, Mass.: Harvard University Press, 1975.

Berthoff, Rowland Tappan. *British Immigrants in Industrial America, 1790–1950*. New York: Russell and Russell, 1953.

Blegen, Theodore C. *Norwegian Migration to America, 1825–1860*. Northfield, Minnesota: The Norwegian-American Historical Association, 1931.

Bogue, Allan G. *Money at Interest*. Lincoln, Nebraska: University of Nebraska Press, 1955.

Boker, H., and F. W. von Bullow. *The Rural Exodus in Czechoslovakia. Studies on Movements of Agricultural Population*. Geneva: International Labor Office, 1935.

Briggs, John W. *An Italian Passage: Immigrants to Three American Cities, 1890–1930*. New Haven: Yale University Press, 1978.

Bubeníček, Rudolf. *Dějiny Čechů v Chicago*. Chicago, Ill.: R. Mejdrich, 1939.

Čapek, Tomáš. *The Czechs (Bohemians) in America: A Study of Their National, Cultural, Political, Social, Economic and Religious Life*. New York: Ams Press, 1969, reprint, orig. 1920.

Carpenter, Niles. *Immigrants and Their Children*. New York: Arno Press and *The New York Times*, 1969.

Cashman, Sean Dennis. *America in the Gilded Age*. New York: New York University Press, 1988.

Československá vlastivěda. Řada II. Národopis. Praha: Sfinx, 1936.

Chambers, Mortimer, et al. *The Western Experience*. 4th ed. New York: Alfred A. Knopf. vol. III: The Modern Era.

Cinel, Dino. *From Italy to San Francisco: The Immigrant Experience*. Stanford, California: Stanford University Press, 1982.

Dvornik, Francis. *Czech Contributions to the Growth of the United States*. Chicago: Benedictine Abbey Press, 1962.

Dvorský, František. *Vlastivěda moravská. II. Místopis. Hrotovský okres*. Brno: Musejní spolek, 1916.

Fleming, D., and B. Bailyn, eds. *Perspectives in American History*, no. 7. Cambridge, Mass.: Charles Warren Center for Studies in American History, 1973.

Forster, Walter O. *Zion on the Mississippi: The Settlement of the Saxon Lutherans in Missouri, 1839–1841*. St. Louis: Concordia Publishing House, 1953.

Fořt, Jan. *O stěhování se lidu našeho do ciziny*. Praha: J. Otto, 1876.

Foster, Robert F. *The Italian Emigration of Our Times.* Cambridge: Harvard University Presss, 1919.

Franěk, Rudolf. *Některé problémy sociálního postavení rolnictva v Čechách na konci 19. a počátku 20. století. Rozpravy Československé Akademie věd, Řada společenských věd, 77, sešit 6.* Praha: Academia, 1967.

Gabaccia, Donna R. *From Sicily to Elizabeth Street: Housing and Social Change Among Italian Immigrants, 1880–1930.* Albany: University of New York Press, 1984.

Garver, Bruce M. "Czech-American Freethinkers on the Great Plains, 1871–1914." In *Ethnicity on the Plains,* ed. Frederick C. Luebke. Lincoln, Nebraska: University of Nebraska Press, 1980.

Gjerde, Jon. *From Peasants to Farmer: The Migration from Balestrand, Norway, to the Upper Middle West.* New York: Cambridge University Press, 1985.

Hábenicht, Jan. *Dějiny Čechův amerických.* St. Louis:—, 1910.

Hájek, Vlastimil. *Poučení pro vystěhovalce do Ameriky.* Praha: Vlast, 1913.

Hansen, Marcus Lee. *The Atlantic Migration, 1607–1860. A History of the Continuing Settlement of the United States.* New York: Harper Torch Books, 1940.

Hoffmannová, Jaroslava. *Vystěhovalectví z Polné do Severní Ameriky ve druhé polovině XIX. století.* Havlíčkův Brod, Czechoslovakia: Vysočina, 1969.

Holmquist, June Drenning, ed. *They Chose Minnesota: A Survey of the State's Ethnic Groups.* St. Paul, Minnesota: Minnesota Historical Society Press, 1981.

Hutchinson, E. P. *Immigrants and Their Children,1850–1950.* New York: John Wiley, 1956.

Hvidt, Kristian. *Flight to America: Social Background of 300,000 Danish Emigrants.* New York: Academic Press, 1975.

Jerome, Harry. *Migration and Business Cycles.* New York: National Bureau of Economic Research, Inc., 1926.

Kamphoefner, Walter D. *The Westfalians: From Germany to Missouri.* Princeton: Princeton University Press, 1987.

Kárníková, Ludmila. *Vývoj obyvatelstva v českých zemích,1754–1914.* Praha: Academia, 1965.

Kašpar, Oldřich. *Tam za mořem je Amerika.* Praha: Československý spisovatel, 1986.

Knittle, Walter Allen. *The Early Eighteenth Century Palantine Emigration: A British Government Redemption Project to Manufacture Naval Stores.* Philadelphia: Philadelphia University, 1936.

Krickens, Richard. *Pursuing the American Dream: White Ethnics and the New Populism.* Bloomington, Indiana: Indiana University Press, 1976.

Kučera, Vladimir, ed. *Czechs and Nebraska.* Lincoln, Nebraska: By the author, 1976.

Kutak, Robert. *The Story of a Bohemian-American Village.* New York: Columbia University Library, 1933; reprint, New York: Arno Press, 1970.

Kutnar, František. *Počátky hromadného vystěhovalectí z Čech v období Bachova absolutismu.* Rozpravy Československé Akademie věd, no. 74, sešit 15. Praha: ČSAV, 1964.

Ledbetter, Eleanor E. *The Czechs of Cleveland.* Cleveland: Americanization Committee, 1919.

Ljungmark, Lars. *Swedish Exodus.* Carbondale, Illinois: Southern Illinois University Press, 1979.

Lucas, Henry S. *Netherlands in America: Dutch Immigration to the United States and Canada, 1789–1950.* Ann Arbor: The University of Michigan Press, 1955.

Lynch, Russell W. *Czech Farmers in Oklahoma.* Stillwater, Oklahoma: Oklahoma Agricultural and Mechanical College Bulletin No. 13, 1942.

McQuillan, Aidan D. *Prevailing Over Time: Ethnic Adjustment on the Kansas Prairies, 1975–1925.* Lincoln: University of Nebraska Press, 1990.

Machan, Clinton, and James W. Mendl. *Krásná Amerika: A Study of the Texas Czechs, 1851–1939.* Austin, Texas: Eakin Press, 1983.

Miller, Kenneth. *The Czechoslovaks in America.* New York: George H. Doran Company, 1922.

Pohl, Josef. *Vylidňování venkova v Čechách v období 1850–1930.* Praha: Masarykova akademie práce, 1922.

Polišenský, Josef, ed. *Začiatky českej a slovenskej emigrácie do USA.* Bratislava: SAV, 1970.

Průcha, Václav, et al. *Hospodářské dějiny Československa v 19. a 20. století.* Praha: nakladatelství Svoboda, 1974.

Rosický, Rose. *A History of Czechs (Bohemians) in Nebraska.* Omaha: Czech Historical Society of Nebraska, 1929.

Runblom, Harold, and Hans Norman, ed. *From Sweden to America: A History of the Migration. A Collective Work of the Uppsala Migration Research Project.* Minneapolis: University of Minnesota Press, 1976.

Šatava, Leoš. *Migrační procesy a české vystěhovalectí 19. století do USA.* Praha: Univesita Karlova, 1989.

Saueressig-Schreuder, Yda. "Dutch Catholic Immigrant Settlement in Wisconsin." In *The Dutch in America: Immigration, Settlement, and Cultural Change,* ed. Robert Swierenga. New Brunswick, New Jersey: Rutgers University Press, 1985.

Shannon, Fred A. *The Farmer's Last Frontier. Agriculture, 1860–1897.* New York: Rinenart & Co., 1945.

Shepperson, W. S. *British Emigration to North America: Projects and Opinions in the Early Victorian Period.* Minneapolis: University of Minnesota Press, 1957.

Schrier, Arnold. *Ireland and the American Emigration, 1850–1900.* New York: Russell and Russell, 1958.

Stovis, Pieter R. D. "Dutch International Migration, 1918–1910." In *The Dutch in America: Immigration, Settlement, and Cultural Change,* ed. Robert Swierenga. New Bruswick, New Jersey: Rutgers University Press, 1985.

Taylor, Philip. *The Distant Magnet: European Emigration to the U.S.A.* New York: Harper & Row Publishers, 1971.

Thernstrom, Stephan, ed. *Harvard Encyclopedia of Ethnic Groups.* Cambridge: Harvard University Press, 1980.

Thomas, Dorothy Swaine. *Social and Economic Aspects of Swedish Population Movements, 1750–1933.* New York: The Macmillan Company, 1941.

Tindall, George Brown. *America: A Narrative History.* 2nd ed. New York: W.W. Norton & Company, 1988.

Urban, Otto. *Česká společnost, 1848–1918.* Praha: Svoboda, 1982.

_____. *Československé dějiny, 1848–1914.* I. Hospodářský a sociální vývoj. Praha: Státní pedagogické nakladatelství, 1988.

Vaněk, Lubomír, and Marie Kapavíková. *Průvodce po archivních fondech a sbírkách.* Kutná Hora: Okresní archív, 1969.

Varlez, -. *Kontinentální vystěhovalecká statistika v Československu.* Praha: Lidová tiskárna, 1925.

Walker, Mack. *Germany and the Emigration, 1816–1885.* Cambridge, Mass.: Harvard University Press, 1984.

ARTICLES IN JOURNALS AND MAGAZINES

Akerman, Sune. "Towards an Understanding of Emigrational Processes." *Scandinavian Journal of History* 3 (1978).

Barborová, Eva. "Vytěhovalectví do Ameriky v Táborském kraji v letech 1855–1862." *Jihočeský sborník historický* XXXV (1–2, 1966).

Berkner, Lutz K. "Rural Family Organization in Europe: A Problem in Comrative History." *Peasant Studies Newsletter* 1 (1972).

Bodnar, John. "Immigration and Modernization: The Case of Slavic Peasants in Industrial America." *Journal of Social History* 10 (1976).

Cironisová, Eva. "Vytěhovalectví z milevského okresu před první světovou válkou." *Jihočeský sborník historický* 49 (1980).

Denney, James. "The Homeland Left Behind." *Magazine of the Midlands* 5 (March 1989).

Doubrava, Ferdinand F. "Experience of a Bohemian Emigration Family." *Wisconsin Magazine of History* (1924).

Ehrenberger, Josef. "Listy z Ameriky a o Rusi." *Hlasy katolického spolku lidového* 6 (Praha), 1870.

Griffith, Martha Eleanor. "The Czechs in Cedar Rapids." *The Iowa Journal of History and Politics* 42 (2 April 1944).

Lom, František. "Vývoj a význam zemědělského tisku v procesu zavádění racionální zemědělské výroby v českých zemích do roku 1914." *Vědecká práce Zemědělského muzea* 25 (1985).

Luebke, Frederick C. "Ethnic Group Settlement on the Great Plains." *Western Historical Quarterly* 8 (October 1977).

———. Review of "From Peasant to Farmers" by Jon Gjerde. In *Minnesota History* (Winter 1985).

Mashek, Nan. "Bohemian Farmers in Wisconsin," *Charities* 13 (3 December 1904).

Ostegren, Robert. "Rattvik to Isanti: A Community Transplanted." Ph.D. diss., University of Minnesota, 1976, quoted in Robert P. Swierenga. "Ethnicity and American Agriculture." *Ohio History* 89 (1980).

Radous, Rudolf. "Z počátků škrobárenského průmyslu v Polné." *Vlastivědný sborník Vysočiny III. Krajské muzeum v Jihlavě. Jihlava* (1959).

Rice, John G., and Robert Ostegren. "The Decision to Emigrate: A Study in Diffusion." *Geografiska Annaler* 60B (1978).

Robek, Antonín. "Korespondence vystěhovalců do Ameriky jako etnografický problém." *Český lid* 71 (1984).

"Seriál o kutnohorských městech a obcích." *Úder* XXI 2 (1 October 1980).

Swierenga, Robert P. "Ethnicity and American Agriculture." *Ohio History* 89 (1980).

Thistlethwaite, Frank. "Migration from Europe Overseas in the Nineteenth and Twentieth Centuries." XIe Congre International des Sciences Historiques, Stockholm, 1960. Rapports, V: Historie Contemporaine.

PERIODICALS

České osady v Americe. 1885, 1886, 1888, 1889, 1891
Hospodář. 1893
Kalendář Amerikán. 1886, 1896, 1897, 1905–1912, 1922
Pokrok Západu. 1873, 1874, 1876–1878, 1881, 1882, 1891

PRIMARY SOURCES

A) Published

United States Government Documents:

U.S. Congress. Senate. U.S. Immigration Commission. *Reports of Immigrants Commission. Immigrants in the Cities.* 61st Cong., 2nd sess., 1911.

U.S. Congress. Senate. U.S. Immigration Commission. *Emigration Conditions in Europe.* 61st Cong., 3rd sess., 5 December–4 March 1911.

U.S. Congress. Senate. U.S. Immigration Commission. *Statistical Review of Immigration, 1820–1910, Distribution of Emigrants, 1850–1900*. 61st Cong., 3rd sess., 1911.
U.S. Congress. Senate. U.S. Immigration Commission. *Distribution of Immigrants, 1850–1900*. 61st Cong., 3rd sess., 1910.
U.S. Congress. Senate. U.S. Immigration Commission. *Immigrants in Industries, 1850–1900*. 61st Cong., 3rd sess., 1910.
Abstract of the Eleventh Census: 1890. Department of the Interior, Census Division. Washington: Government Printing Office, 1896.
U.S. Census Office, *Schedules of the Nebraska State Census of 1885*.

Auerhan, Jan, Jan Hejret, and Alois Svojsík. *Anketa o českém vystěhovalectí uspořadaná zahraničním odborem národní rady české*. Praha: Nákladem Národní rady české, 1912.
Cox, E. Evelyn. *1870 Nebraska Census*. vol. 1. Ellensberg, Washington: Ancestree House, 1979.
Sedmnáctá zpráva o činnosti českého odboru rady zemědělské pro Království české za rok 1908. Praha: Rolnická tiskárna a nakladatelství, 1909.
Swierenga, Robert P. "Dutch Patterns of Migration to the United States in the Mid-Nineteenth Century." St. Paul, Minn.: Immigration History Research Center, 1986. [photocopy]
Výsledky šetření (Agrární anketa) poměrů hospodářských i kulturních zemědělského obyvatelstva v království českém v letech 1898–1900: Z původních prací vyšetřujících komisařů. Praha: Zemědělská rada pro království české, 1914.

B) Unpublished

Manuscripts:

Bergman, Marion. "America's Slavic Legacy." MS, 1975. IHRC.
"Czech Immigrant Passenger List (For Nebraska), 1879." Comp. Margie Sobotka. Omaha: Czech Historical Society of Nebraska, 1982.
Haudek, Elsie, ed. "The History of Frank and Teresia (Chapek) Benes." Weston, Nebraska: By the author, 1985.
Kořalka, Jiří, and Květa Kořalková. "Tchecoslovaquie. Basic Features of Mass Emigration from the Czech Lands During the Capitalist Era, 1980(?)." TMs [photocopy]. Received from the authors.
Mareš, Frank. "Nebraska, Kansas Czech Settlers, 1891–1895." Comp. Margie Sobotka. Omaha: Nebraska State Historical Society.
Polišenský, Josef. "Obecné problémy dějin českého vystěhovalectí, 1850–1914." 1987 TMs [photocopy]. Received from the author.
Šatava, L. "K problematice formování a stabilizace českého etnika v USA (1848–1914)." MS received from Nebraska State Historical Society (David Murphy).

Archival material:

Personal archive of author

Čeledínská knížka. Issued in the village of Slatina (29 March 1885). The book belonged to Bartoloměj Flaštín, Slatina u Klatov. In possession of Elmer Kral, Grand Island, Nebraska.

Bremen Archive

"Father Franz Prachař in Bremen." St. Raphael-Blatt XXVI (3, 1911). Veroffentlichungen aus dem Staatsarchiv der Freien Hansestadt Bremen, 2-P.8.B.8.c.Bd.2 Nr.36.

"From the speech of St. Raphael representatives as the gathering of catholics in Mainz in 1911." St. Raphael-Blatt XXVI (3 1911) Veroffentlichungen aus dem Staatsarchiv der Reien Hansestadt Bremen.

Brno State District Archive

Appendix to Bača, 6023/1225, M3354.

Immigration History Research Center

Minneapolis, Minnesota. Rypka, Zdenka. MS Collection, Box 1. Immigration History Research Center.

Kutná Hora District Archive

The District Police Administration Records.

"Hlavní kniha domovních listů, 1874–1919." Kniha č.9. Fond OÚ.

Okresní úřad Čáslav, 1855–1945 (1948)—inventář, Okresní archív, Kutná Hora

Pamětní kniha, obec Velký Lomeč, 1923. Okresní archív Kutná Hora, 1850–1945.

Pamětní kniha, obec Kluky.

Písek District Archive

Fond OU Tábor, k.165.

Fond OU Milevsko, k.35.

University of Chicago Archive

"Czechs and Slovaks Living Abroad." Special Collection. Čapek Papers. Box 14-Series 4-d.

Vienna State Archive

The Austro-Hungarian Consul, New Orleans, to the Ministry of Foreign Affairs, 19 February 1871. 22/10/V. 2 F15, Aus u. Einwanderung 1870–79, Auswanderung 1880–1918. 1/1-15, fol.1–64, 25/IV 31. I/38a akten von 1870 bis 1879.

The Charge D'Affairs of Austria Frankenstein, Washington, to the Secretary of State Seward, 16 January 1868. Admin. Reg. F. 15/1 folium 106r–117r.

The Senate Commissioner for the Foreign Affairs of Bremen, to the Governor in Prague, 11 September 1869. Admin. Reg. F. 15/1 folium 106r–117r, Vienna Archive.

Library of Náprstek Muzeum

Scrapbook "Čechové mimo vlast" (Czechs living abroad). II, IV, V, IX, XI, XII, XIII, XV, XVI, XVII,

Theses or Dissertations:

Fimple, Kathleen L. "An Analysis of the Changing Spatial Dimensions of Ethnic Neighborhoods in Omaha, Nebraska, 1880–1900." Ph.D. diss., University of Nebraska, 1989.

Fisher, Joe A. "The Liquor Question in Nebraska, 1880–1890." M.A. thesis, University of Nebraska, 1952.

Kleinschmidt, John R. "The Political Behavior of the Bohemian and Swedish Ethnic Groups in Nebraska, 1884–1900." M.A. thesis, University of Nebraska, 1968.

Kubecek, Clarence John. "The Czechs of Butler County, 1870–1940." M.A. thesis, University of Nebraska, 1958.

Sellin, Loyd Bernard. "The Settlement of Nebraska to 1880." M.A. thesis, University of South Carolina, 1940.

Van Hoff, Joseph John. "A History of the Czechs of Knox County, Nebraska." M.A. thesis, University of Nebraska, 1938.

Varejcka, Janet. "The Czech Immigrant—A Process of Acculturation: Schuyler, Nebraska, 1870–1920." M.A. thesis, University of Nebraska, 1977.

Personal archive of the author and guide books of the emigration areas were consulted.

Index

About the Author

Born April 12, 1956, in Prague, Czechoslovakia, Štěpánka Korytová-Magstadt grew up and began her higher education in that city. She won a general-knowledge competition on the national (Czechoslovak) level and was awarded a trip to Kiev and Soviet Central Asia in 1975. She received the Elizabeth Nuffield Scholarship, which enabled her to study in England, where she was awarded a B.A. Honors from the University of Southampton in 1982.

Ms. Korytová then came to the United States, where she completed her M.A. in Education at the University of Nebraska in Kearney in 1984. She began her Ph.D. course work there, in history, and passed her comprehensive examinations there in 1986. Returning to Czechoslovakia, she completed her Ph.D. at Charles University, where she received that degree in 1991. Her dissertation was entitled "Czech Rural Immigration and Settlement in Nebraska, 1860–1900." That work formed the basis for the present book.

Proficient in Russian, English, and—of course—Czech, Dr. Korytová has done extensive translating and teaching in those languages. She has also won numerous awards and scholarships.

Now married and the mother of a son, Michael, Dr. Korytová-Magstadt presently lives in Kearney, Nebraska.

To order

Name_____

Address _____

City_____ State_____ Zip_____

Qty _____ Paper ($14.95) $ _____
       _____ Hardcover ($24.95) $ _____
              Sales tax (IA res only—5%) $ _____
              Shipping & Handling—U.S.
                 (First copy at $3.00 per
                 copy, additional copies at
                 $1.50 per copy) $ _____
              Total Cost $ _____

Check or money order enclosed $ _____

☐ Mastercard ☐ Visa Credit Card #_____

    Exp Date _____ Phone _____

Send to:
    Rudi Publishing
    Distribution Center
    153 38th St. NE
    Cedar Rapids, Iowa 52402

Make checks payable to Rudi Publishing. To order by phone (credit
card orders only), call **toll free 1-800-999-6901.**